Direct Experience, Real Spirituality,
and Wednesday Afternoons

THE
EVERY
DAY
MYSTIC

Edited by
KEVIN SWEENEY

First Edition

Cover design and interior layout by Matthew J. Distefano

Print ISBN 978-1-964252-29-2
Electronic ISBN 978-1-964252-30-8
Printed in the United States of America

Published by Quoir
Chico, California
www.quoir.com

CONTENTS

FOREWORD
Dr. Carmen Acevedo Butcher

I GREW UP IN Georgia, outdoors mostly. Partly because summer was a sauna and we had no air conditioning so out was cooler than in. Earth herself/himself/itself/themself was my first teacher of mystery. This dirt, sky, creek, and sun-drenched temple introduced me to the temple within me of grounded, soaring, flowing, and luminous silence, which began healing and companioning me out into the world with compassion, and that for me is contemplation aka everyday mysticism.

Even when the dreaded chore was raking up pine needles, I sensed creation's welcome. The susurration of the morning wind in the upper evergreen branches of tall loblolly pines spoke peace in young me as my sneakers made soft footsteps over the brown carpet of pine straw. Rake in hand, I felt interconnectedness.

I also walked through woods and fields as escape from my father's undiagnosed illness. Home became a loud, risky, violent place. Too, playdates could be unpredictable for a sun-kissed, olive-skinned, mixed-race kid whose brownness stood out. One such ended when out of the blue I was punched in the mouth, a front tooth chipped by someone who'd acted like she wanted to be my friend. Wandering the fields, with red-tailed hawks as my companions, my soul heard and wordlessly rested in the oneing silence.

This awareness is an ancient experience. Chief siʔaɫ (Seattle), leader of the Duwamish, Suquamish, and other Puget Sound tribes, describes life's everyday mystical interweaves: "This we know, all things are connected like the blood which unites one family. All things are connected" (duwamishtribe.org). In Ordinary Mysticism Mirabai Starr sings of our interbeing and belonging: "Ours is a time of collective awakening, of reciprocity, of active participation in the web of interbeing."

It has taken me a long time to be able to admit how deeply I relate to Mary Oliver's openness: "I got saved by the beauty of the world." Because our culture doesn't encourage us to be poets at heart.

This book does. Its gentle wisdom invites us to question, open, let go of all that no longer supports us, befriend ourselves and each other, and honor who we are. This collection of our stories feels like a kind conversation between friends and you're invited to join. And add your own.

If you grew up in a world where God was synonymous with certitude, as I did, Everyday Mysticism may feel like a bracing sea breeze. If sermons were shouted at you in packed pews, and the redder the face, the angrier God was at humans, this book's insights may sound like Welcome home on a cold winter day, a bowl of steaming homemade soup set on the table for you. If you were raised on dogma, original sin, and penal substitutionary atonement theory, these stories' gentle sagacity may at first feel transgressive as it frees the joy of asking open-ended questions, living into original blessing, and experiencing the life-and-death of Jesus as "a revelation of the infinite and participatory love of God," as Richard Rohr says in The Universal Christ.

Everyday Mysticism includes everyone, of course. Its stories remind us that we don't have to be a monk, nun, priest, or somehow "good enough" to participate in meditation. We also don't have to wait until we're more healed or fully understand what mysticism means. After all, who really can explain it, anyway?

These chapters model listening to inner tugs, inviting more awe into our lives, and embracing "the art of seeing" prized by Carl Jung (Collected Works). Diving deep into practices, they keep it real. One shares starting a Centering Prayer practice "within the vestibule" of a Nissan Altima on lunch breaks and describes lectio divina or Scripture- steeping as "letting ourselves be read."

This collection asks the questions that matter. How do I know God loves me? How can we live in a world of suffering and of social media where internet connections threaten real interconnectedness? What does it mean to be human in a world of increasing illusions? Is mysticism just a mind game, or does it move us toward real healing and alleviating the world's pain? Where does meditation connect with being anti-racist? Why is mysticism often in conflict with dominant institutions and systems? Does Christian mysticism dialogue well with mysticism in other faith and wisdom traditions? How do we walk, or even dance along the mystic path? How can we meditate without ceasing? How can we handle hatred and become liberated together? How can we like Hagar see ourselves as God sees us? How can each of us recognize our real name at the center of our being?

Here you encounter fellow seekers dancing with discovering vocabulary for everyday mystical experiences as they listen to and take seriously the movements of their own souls and lives. While these stories take inspiration from past and present mystics and creatives, including Brother Lawrence, Howard Thurman, Thomas Merton, James Finley, bell hooks, Rabbi Abraham Joshua Heschel, Gospel of Thomas, Lama Rod Owens, Teresa of Avila, Hildegard of Bingen, Dorothy Day,

Desmond Tutu, Thich Nhat Hanh, Maya Angelou, Lerita Coleman Brown, Bernadette Roberts, Therese Taylor- Stinson, Grace Ji Sun Kim, Octavia Butler, Meister Eckhart, the Cloud of Unknowing's Anonymous, John Coltrane, and Dr. Barbara A. Holmes, among others, they return us again and again to the divine within each soul.

May we recognize-and-realize this now, together.

INTRODUCTION
Kevin Sweeney

MYSTICS ARE MYSTERIOUS AREN'T they?

They seem to pop up sporadically across cultures and eras, while beautifully transcending and challenging conventional forms of seeing wherever they are. They say wholehearted yeses to questions other people haven't even started asking yet. They proclaim defiant noes to the uncritically accepted structure of their spiritual and social versions of the status quo. They don't ever fully fit into the expected shape of their time and place, and yet still aways seem to feel at home.

And what do they always do in their unique and respective points in history?

They offer wisdom.

They share poetry.

They write.

(And we also never really know what they do for work or how they pay the bills.)

Naturally, their message is always carried in a contextually shaped container, but the content within always seems to be made up of the same substances.

Awe.

Gratitude.

Peace.

Joy.

Grace.

Acceptance.

And of course, and especially, love.

Over 2,000 years ago in the Ancient Near East, a young man David who would eventually become King of Israel wrote, "Remember, Lord, Your compassion, and your faithful love, for they have existed from antiquity." (Psalm 25:6)

Rumi, a 13th Century Sufi mystic from Iran shared, "Be certain in the religion of Love, there are no believers or unbelievers. Love embraces all."

St. Hildegard of Bingen, a 12th Century German Benedictine Abbess stated, "Love abounds in all things, excels from the depths to beyond the stars, is lovingly disposed to all things."

And Thomas Merton, an American Catholic monk living in the mid 20th Century claimed that, "The root of Christian love is not the will to love, but the faith that one is loved."

Each of these profound mystics and prolific writers were living and working thousands of years apart and speaking different languages, and somehow they were still harmoniously singing the ever-present song of Love. With different languages, they spoke the same Language.

With different voices, they spoke with One Voice. And with different messages, they shared the same Message.

Along with the shared foundation of infinite love they all stand on, mystics also share a kind of playfulness. They live out of a spacious freedom that can be interpreted as naïve, or even reckless. Some may assume there is no way these mystical tricksters have faced the the seriousness of human suffering based on the poetic and whimsical sayings they espouse. But these powerful voices have learned the trick that if you take life absolutely seriously, you don't have to take it seriously at all.

Mystics are swimming in the deep end while most people are still comfortable wading in the shallow waters of the kiddie pool.

Mystics are laughing in the middle of a world that is burning, while most people are still figuring out what to do with their anger and despair.

Mystics keep responding with stories, art, and poetry while the so called serious people are looking for conceptual answers and certainty.

Mystics challenge us, inspire us, and invite us further into a life we do not always understand, but still want more of.

But all of this raises the question:

What does any of this mystical stuff have to do with a regular Wednesday afternoon?

· · · · ● · · ● · · · ·

THE AFOREMENTIONED QUESTION IS about the practical nature of mysticism.

It speaks of our desire to know exactly how direct experience of God and a conscious experience of the Unity of All Things transforms and translates into our real lives. Genuine exiles from institutional religion need to know how the movement toward the mystical liberates how they move with everything else. Or, to re-state the question: what does mysticism have to do with a Wednesday afternoon?

One of the reasons for this book is because the answer is...

Well.

Everything.

Nothing is more grounding and practical than the mystical. The immediate knowing of the Divine and the organic transformation that happens within this union does not simply change how I see the world, it transfigures the very "I" that is doing the seeing. Most religion gives you a different way of seeing and translating reality, real awakening and union with Christ liberates and transforms you in your own awareness and being.

When you are perpetually seen by an Affirmative Presence, you no longer need others to see you in order to be validated.

When you experience a Love that, by nature, leads you to increasing wholeness, you no longer look to any other human being to make you whole.

When you recognize your Supreme Identity is Eternal and Infinite, you no longer have to identify with any of the momentary disguises of the ego to feel secure.

So yes.

It changes everything.

And to ground this experience even more for those Wednesday afternoon moments, let's get even more down-to-earth.

The mystical is why we can take one big settling breath while buckling our kids into their car seats without losing our shit. Identification with Love is why we can recognize and resist the impulse to defend ourselves in real time when we are being misrepresented, because instead of justifying ourselves to others, we've learned how to let go into the hidden and validating Presence of God. Real awakening is the reason we can truly celebrate other people's success because we inherently trust that their addition to the world does not subtract anything from the essence of who we are. Union with Christ is why we can embody the humility required to take ownership of our mistakes, because even in the vulnerability of those moments, we know we are safe. And the interior spaciousness that opens up through immediate knowing is what allows us to let our partner have the last word, instead of firing off one more comment that will lead us further away from each other.

Those are just a few examples of the what a liberated life—that only comes from direct experience of God and not just beliefs about God—feels like in our everyday life. Proof of the mystical experience is always and only the embodiment of love, and the millions of ways it manifests in the concreteness of our lives.

With that in mind, each chapter in this book is an answer to the question about how the movement toward to the mystical is incarnated in our own lives on those Wednesday afternoons. This is why you will read about intuition, pausing, mantras, breathing, trusting our own seeing, interpreting the sacred text of our own lives, creativity, speaking truth to power, not abandoning the real world, courageously leaving old spaces, and many other experiences.

The offering of wisdom from these leading voices in this book is born out of the nexus where the depth of suffering becomes the delight of joy. Remember, the mystics are who they are because they have felt pain so deeply. They also have become who they have become because they have stayed with the pain long enough until it had no choice to but to metamorphose into awakening.

For these everyday mystics,

it's not jus learning, it's living,

it's not just believing, it's becoming,

it's not just explanation, it's embodiment.

The luminous mystic Adyashanti wrote, "So the whole Jesus Story, ultimately, is the map of a journey that happens within us."

So my hope is that through the journeys that are being shared in these pages, you will gain more clarity of the journey that is unfolding in and through you.

1
MYSTICISM AS A HEART POSTURE
Aurelia Dávila Pratt

THE POSTURE

MYSTICISM IS NOT RESERVED for the good at meditating, the good at faith, or the good enough. Mysticism isn't reserved for priests, monks, spiritual leaders, or the extra holy. It is not an achievement or a gift that only some receive. Instead, it is a spiritual muscle to be strengthened; a spiritual tool to be sharpened. It is fertile soil that requires our tending.

Mysticism is a posture our heart takes, and any heart can take it.

How does mysticism fit into our everyday lives? No one else can answer this question for us. Instead, to discover our answer(s), we must make room within ourselves.

We must cultivate within us a spaciousness, an expansion of our spiritual capacities. Instead of confining ourselves to the limiting frameworks of thinking and knowing, we spread out in the liberative flow of mystery, where Divine intuition guides our being.

For many of us, our faith journeys have been limited to external forms of approval in order to be considered valid. We are granted permission to appeal to tradition (a reflection of those in power throughout church history), to reason (approval from the academic or spiritually influential), and to scripture (approved interpretations reserved for a select few).

We have an abundance of external voices guiding our faith journeys, but the internal voice is tossed aside. Our intuition and experiences are downplayed or altogether disregarded. Tragically, we become dependent on external sources to solely guide and shape our faiths.

Yet, we are made in God's image. God dwells within us and in all our experiences. Mysticism invites us to take a posture that acknowledges this. It is a posture our heart takes daily, but we cannot learn to take it without the guidance of our intuition.

But how can we experience consistent Divine connection if we've been trained to be suspicious of our own internal voice? How do we break free from such a limiting faith that is totally reliant upon others? Here is what we do:

Daily, we commit to the work of attention. We pay close attention to what our inner voice is trying to tell us. We honor the cues of our bodies. We learn to embrace mystery and all the beautiful gifts that come with it. We listen to the rhythm of our lives, and in doing so, we become students of nuance, paradox, and non-dualism.

At first, it will seem overwhelming because there isn't a one-size-fits-all blueprint. There is only our willingness to accept the Spirit-assignment given to each of us: pay attention, listen, and begin again as often is needed. To commit to such a path is to choose the mystical heart posture. And it's not that we can't do it. It's just that these muscles have not (yet!) been worked out and strengthened.

Once again we must remind ourselves that mysticism is not reserved for the spiritually elite or the naturally inclined to contemplation. We just need a little bit of room to work out our spiritual muscles. The strength developing is what creates spaciousness within us. We need this expanded capacity to embody the truth that mysticism is for us, too.

This awareness is enough to change our lives. In order to access such awareness, we do not need a certain personality or even years of practice. If we need anything, perhaps it is lightheartedness, a willingness to be playful, to laugh, to hold things lightly, and to prioritize things like awe, wonder and gratitude. Lightheartedness is our pathway to the posture, a daily awareness that God is already with us. We can directly connect with God in all moments.

From our expanded capacities, we make room within us for lightheartedness. As we do so, we toss the deadweight—the "spiritual" stuff that does not serve us (which is not spiritual stuff at all!). We throw out things like shame, notions of success, religious rigidity, and so on. You know what you need to throw out.

With lightheartedness in tow and the spaciousness within us ever-expanding, we become mystics who, in Fr. Rohr's words "have nothing to prove and nothing to protect. I am who I am and it's enough." We are who we are and it's enough.

We are not defined by our success, our religious piety, or even our doctrine. Rather, we are mystics because of the heart posture we choose to take every single ordinary day.

QUOTIDIAN

I'm willing to bet I'm not the only one who has ever wondered, "Is it me, or is it God?" Was that nudge, that thought, that call to action coming from me, or was it coming from God?

What draws me to mysticism is the realization that I don't need to answer this age old question. Or if I must, perhaps the answer is yes, or perhaps it is both.

The point is that something is not right with the question itself. If anything, it reveals the binary thinking that lives below the surface of many Christian paradigms. These are rigid paradigms that split the soul from the body, making the soul good and the body bad. Spirit: good. Flesh: bad. Spirit: God. Flesh: Us. God is good. We are inherently bad.

Within this paradigm, it is hammered into us that our bodies, hearts, inclinations, and instincts are deceitful and beyond cure. So when the question arises, "Is it me, or is it God?" our discernment is conflated with the harmful messaging that has been drilled into us that we cannot be trusted.

Instead of exploring our Spirit-intuition, we entrust it to others. We hand over our ability to experience direct Divine connection to those we perceive to be holier, more enlightened, or more knowledgeable. We seek out faith leaders to tell us how to proceed. We give up our soul autonomy and appeal to the interpretation and approval of external forces, to the detriment of our internal voice.

Bit by bit, we disconnect from our ability to recognize Spirit nudges in our instincts, creativity, sense of wonder, and our bodies' cues. We disconnect from our ability to hear from and connect to God. The truth that we are empowered via imago Dei (God in us) to have consistent, direct Divine experience becomes a box of forgotten memories, dusted over on the highest shelf in the basement of our souls.

There it lays, but there it can be reclaimed.

Eventually I woke up to the tragedy of my own fragmented faith. I looked deeply into my soul through the lens of my very own life, and I remembered. I dusted off the box. I collected the pieces of my faith that had once been doled out to others.

In the ordinary, I reclaimed the right to my own spiritual work and to my ability to directly experience the things of God. Quotidian as my entry point, I found rest and a home in the mystical.

The first time I encountered the concept of quotidian was in a sermon. The message in a nutshell was the little things are the big things. Indeed, quotidian means ordinary or everyday, especially when mundane. God is found in the quotidian details of our everyday lives. God is present amid our everyday tasks, everyday moments, and within everyday people. God is already with us, no conditions or prerequisites required.

This concept changed me, or perhaps a better way to say it is quotidian helped me return. It brought me back to the faith of my childhood, which was an intuitive, instinctive faith that did not require approval or explanation. Quotidian reawakened me to a firm faith foundation that I had once embodied, before all the doctrine and people pleasing took over.

Many books have been written on this concept that the sacred can be found in the ordinary. Hallelujah, this is no longer a novel idea! The writing that most shaped my life was Quotidian Mysteries: Laundry, Liturgy, and "Women's Work" by Kathleen Norris.

This essay introduced me to the simple, yet profound truth that God was with me, particularly in the necessary ritual of my daily chores. The author, Kathleen Norris, reflected on her experience attending a Catholic wedding, having not been in a church service in many years.

"I found it remarkable— and still find it remarkable—that in that big, fancy church, after all of the dress-up and the formalities of the wedding mass, homage was being paid to the lowly truth that we human beings must wash the dishes after we eat and drink. The chalice, which had held the very blood of Christ, was no exception. And I found it enormously comforting to see the priest as a kind of daft housewife, overdressed for the kitchen, in bulky robes, puttering about the altar, washing up after having served so great a meal to so many people. It brought the mass home to me and gave it meaning."

Norris connected this moment with the ritual of daily chores and tasks, ones that are often unenjoyed and under appreciated. It brings to mind the 17th century monk and mystic, Brother Lawrence, who for thirty years labored in the monastery kitchens as his daily work. Known for his prayer posture called practicing the Presence of God, Brother Lawrence looked upon his kitchen duties with reverence and gratitude.

"When I began my tasks, I said to God with a child-like trust: "My God, since you are with me, and since you ask me to apply my mind to these external duties, I beg you, give me the grace to remain with you and keep you company."

Both Norris and Brother Lawrence found God not only in the mundane moments, but perhaps especially among them. This constant access to the presence of God is the essence of the Christian mystical tradition. We don't have to do anything spectacular for God to be known to us every single ordinary day.

This realization transformed my life. Like most ordinary moments, it wasn't a sudden transformation. If anything, it was more like that famous Karate Kid scene where Mr. Miyagi requires Daniel to do all sorts of menial chores before he will teach him the art of karate. Wax on, wax off and over time, Daniel realizes he has built up a certain muscle memory he could call upon.

The mystic's posture helps us recall a muscle memory we have within us to directly connect with and experience God at any given moment of our days. This mystery of faith, in which we live and breathe God, dwells outside of logical explanation.

This is why a mystical faith is necessary. This is why mysticism is for all of us. More than anything, our quotidian, ordinary moments want to remind us of this, if only we are willing to pay attention.

THE MYSTIC CHILD

In the early 90s, my family attended a small Catholic church in the rural North Louisiana town where I grew up. The Catholic presence in our town was small, and our tiny church was a reflection of this. The property consisted of three small buildings: a simple, white parsonage, the church building, and basement space that served as the fellowship hall, which we entered by walking down the sidewalk that wrapped around the side of the church building.

Upon entering the small church, rows of pews immediately filled the room. One center aisle led to the altar and the sanctuary space surrounding it. On either side of the sanctuary, there were entrances to two smaller rooms. The entrance to the left of the altar was where congregants participating in the mass might prepare. When I became an altar server a few years later, it was where I would robe up. The entrance on the right led to the priest's office and to a cramped, but cozy study that doubled as a waiting area.

In the study, rows of Bibles and catholic education books lined one wall, and a chair or two was nestled among the books. The only thing separating it from the priest's office was the confessional, which was built into the wall, creating a sort of hallway that separated office and study.

One day, when I was 7 or 8 years old, my parents had a meeting with the priest. I was left to my own devices in the small study area. Only "devices" weren't really a thing in the early 1990s. So while the meeting was likely only an hour or less, in my kid-brain it seemed to go on forever. Out of pure, desperate boredom, I turned my attention to the books.

I scanned the shelves, looking for anything that might pique my interest. There wasn't much by way of children's books, but I was a good reader and quickly found myself intrigued by a book that must have been for youth because the cover held an image of what appeared to be a teen-aged girl. I can't remember the title, only that this was my first time encountering the word "mystic".

Curious, I opened and began reading about a girl and her incredible encounters with God. Sprawled out on the carpet of the tiny Catholic study, I read about the mystics and their wonder-filled Divine experiences.

Truly, this moment was a catalyst for me. It cultivated within me an openness and eagerness concerning the presence of God. Though I didn't fully understand it right away, it gifted me with an endearment and interest toward the mystic's path. It shaped the beginnings of a posture that would go with me throughout my life, one that would be ready and receptive to future Divine encounters.

More than anything, it offered the encouraging realization that it could be me. God could be present with me. After all, the story I happened upon that day was about a young girl. Mary, revered in the Catholic church, was also a young girl. And I was a young girl!

I put it all together, and in that moment a foundation was laid, one that confirmed spiritual truths were accessible to me, no doubt about it. This foundation provided me with comforting knowledge of God's presence, within me and around me. It strengthened and solidified my faith, and this mystical faith would go with me and support me for years to come, unexplainable but undeniable.

As a college student, when I left the Catholic church in favor of the Baptist tradition, it was still there. As I fell deeply into the grips of evangelical fundamentalism, it lay dormant, but ever present. When I was deep in faith crisis in seminary and just after, it held me up. When I finally collected those long forgotten faith-pieces at a Catholic monastery years later, it kindly greeted me, "hello, old friend. I'm still here."

Amid deconstruction, faith reclamation and continued evolving and re-imagining, this mystical faith foundation has remained my steady ground. Here's the thing: it can be steady ground for all of us.

THE PARADOX

Research shows that the physical practice of grounding includes reduced inflammation and pain, improved sleep, improved response to trauma, accelerated healing, and improved blood flow.

This means we should make direct contact with the ground as much as possible, quite literally for the sake of our healing. We put our feet in the surf, in the grass, in the dirt. We touch the earth; we connect to what is around us, understanding that is within us, too. Perhaps this is what it means to say "You are dust, and to dust you shall return." We are connected to the earth and to all of creation. Physically connecting with this truth as often as we can will make a difference in our lives.

Mysticism is a heart posture we can choose to take each day. It is spiritual grounding, in which we tend to our inner landscape, and the healing it offers us is plentiful. The benefits include reduced inflammation (stress), less pain (suffering), more rest (peace), an improved response to our circumstances (including our traumas), and improved flow (connection with Spirit within us).

Because the paradox is this: the heart posture is both grounding and flow at once. It grounds us, granting us a steadiness to face the realities of our lives. Despite chaos, disappointment, stress, loss, grief, uncertainty, we are on solid ground.

Simultaneously, this posture involves a willingness to move in alignment with Spirit flow. The reality is we are always changing, the world is always changing, and every day is different. If we can count on anything, all the time, we can count on change. So then, for us to be well and to know peace, it is essential that we go with the Flow. Could this be what it means to surrender?

The heart posture is both grounding and flow at once. It is the firm foundation we can count on, and it is our teacher in the art of loose grips. Even as we stand on steady ground, we hold everything lightly here, ready to follow the Spirit energy that moves us. Our ability to hold this paradox requires a connection to our God-given intuition. It requires our trust that Spirit speaks to and through us. This is the gift of mysticism. It offers the spaciousness we need to cultivate this trust.

As everyday mystics, we are empowered to follow the Spirit cues, those nudges leading us to guidance and clarity, revealing God's presence in and around us. Our practice ground is our everyday life, and the very roots of mysticism means that we don't always have to explain this logically. We can simply stop thinking and doing and instead be present in the beauty of the mystery.

The mystery of faith is a choice. It is deep, daily spiritual work through the simple act of listening to our lives. It is consistency and practice. It is "failing" and then patiently beginning again. It is tenderness and self compassion. It is a reconnection and a re-orientation to our truest path. Here, all the pieces of our lives are integrated. Internal and external are integrated.

Our daily willingness to posture our hearts toward the mystical is like returning to a well of spiritual nourishment. The well exists, but we must choose to come. The well exists, but we must choose to drink. One cup is not enough. We need hydration every single day. This is what I mean when I say to be a mystic is not to do a, b, or c. It is a heart-posture only you can choose to take. Only you can choose to show up. Only you can choose to drink. So drink, and drink deeply, daily.

We prioritize this inner posture for the sake of our wellness and thriving so that we can face the world well and whole. Prioritizing this posture is not meant to be an escape from the world. Rather, it is our sustenance so that we can be full participants, stewards and helpers and activists who pour out with energy and joy.

Too many goodhearted people show up to our collective work parched and empty, only to burn out and cave to hopelessness and despair. It is not sustainable. If we are going to have any impact, we must be people who have access to our own spiritual well. We must prioritize this paradox posture that is both grounding and flow.

So here is what we do: we practice the posture. Day by day. Moment by moment. Inch by inch. Wax on; wax off. Over time, our muscle memory will strengthen. Our spiritual capacity will deepen. We expand. In fullness, we show up to the well and to the world. Another beautiful paradox. Daily, we show up with courage and love.

We get rattled; we get shaken. We lose hope, and peace feels impossible. The rough waters of life toss and turn us every which way. Relationships and emotions cause suffering and upheaval. We get disconnected and disoriented and then... we return. We re-connect and re-orient. With patience and without shame, we settle back into our posture. We drink from our well.

There's no such thing as failure. There is only practice. Now, let's begin. And then, inevitably, begin again.

2

SURRENDERING TO THE SACRED: A CONTEMPLATIVE JOURNEY

Tia Norman

JESUS SAYS:

If those who lead you say to you: "Look, the kingdom is in the sky!" then the birds of the sky will precede you.

If they say to you: "It is in the sea," then the fishes will precede you.

Rather, the kingdom is inside of you and outside of you.

When you come to know yourselves, then you will be known, and you will realize that you are the children of the living Father.

The Gospel of Thomas, 3:1-4

I didn't want to be here anymore and I knew I needed help. I was 18 years old and on the verge of graduating from high school. The knowledge of the dysfunction and dangers in my home had seeped outside of the walls and into the streets of the small West Texas town I lived in, placing me in a fishbowl. My friends, their parents, teachers, and even strangers knew what was going on with my family. My household was no longer a safe place and a friend's family agreed to take me in while I finished school.

On this particular day, the day I felt like I didn't want to be here anymore, I was alone in the house. I don't remember if it was a teacher or a police officer who had given me the small card with a phone number to a helpline on it - I just knew I needed help. I dialed the number and there was no answer. This sent me into further despair, amplified by the thought that I couldn't even get help right. I hung up the phone, my body collapsed and I cried out, "HELP ME!"

Everything changed in that moment.

The world became completely still and I had a deep sense, a knowing, that I was being held. I could feel a Presence with me. There in that moment of surrender, in that moment of desperation and chaos, I felt peace and I knew that no matter the circumstances I would be ok. I knew what I felt was God.

This experience is important to know about my background, my spiritual formation, and my deeply held conviction that what is often searched for within our religious institutions and the complementing educational systems as a means to fulfill our spiritual longings resides predominantly in the constitution of our being. We all have access to the Divine.

It is that access that changes worlds. It is that access that equips us to speak truth to power. The mystic knows this.

I finished high school, left one Texas town for another, and went on to college. I've been married and divorced. I've been in love and been betrayed. I've held my two babies and watched them grow into young adults. I've followed what seemed like the perfect career path only to discover that the Presence I felt holding me in that room as a teenager would make itself known again; tugging me toward a new vocation. In this instance, I wasn't so inclined to surrender. I have discovered if I don't trust the tug, eventually, it intensifies into what feels like a push.

My dream job in sports marketing was unfolding while something within me was unraveling. I thought I was going crazy. I felt "called to ministry" and had no idea what that meant. I had diligently worked my way up the corporate ladder and the urge to explore another path continued to beckon. It was almost as if I was being taunted to leap from the rung I was perched on. It made no sense.

Why would I, of all people, be called to ministry?

Yes, I had a mystical experience as a teenager but that hardly seemed like a prerequisite to making such a drastic change. I wasn't raised in church. Certainly, someone with a stronger background, education, and training would make more sense than me.

My church attendance had mostly been reserved for the occasional Catholic Mass when visiting my mother's side of the family as a child. I often found myself confused by the structure of the service and displaced when the invitation for communion came as the bread and wine were expressly intended for those who believed "in one, holy, catholic and apostolic church." I never knew exactly what to do during those Eucharistic moments. I opted to stay in the pew as the rows of congregants stood and made their way to the wafers and cups. I knew I believed in God but I wasn't sure about believing in a God that didn't seem to be welcoming all to the table.

My sporadic journeys to Mass were countered by even more infrequent visits to church with my granny. Granny was my father's mother and she attended a Baptist church. Joining her was usually reserved for Easter. One must understand that you didn't show up to granny's church looking any kind of way. No. I remember many Sundays listening to gospel music flow from her old AM/FM radio as she got ready for service. There were stockings and girdles, there were fine fabrics and jewels. There was perfume and there were purses with matching shoes. Her outfits would come to completion with the placement of a beautiful hat gently atop her silver curls. As a child my wardrobe did not house anything as extravagant as the likes of granny's, so for me, Easter Sunday with her also meant a trip to the department store for the two of us. It meant a new dress, new tights, new shoes, and when I was old enough it meant a purse to match the kitten heels on my feet. Most of my church memories with her had everything to do with preparing to go into the building and not much to do with what was happening inside the building itself.

The spiritual space between the periodic Mass and Easter Sunday preparations was filled in at home. My mother made it clear when I was very young that there were things within her Catholic upbringing she disagreed with. Meanwhile, my friends were sharing experiences connected to certain denominational rites of passage. I asked Mom what our religion was and she stated that she wanted me to "choose for myself." *Now I lay me down to sleep* was a prayer she frequently guided me through as a child and served as an opening to the idea that I could talk to God. I carried that notion with me into adulthood and into the sense that I was being called to a new line of work. Certainly,

God wasn't now trying to engage in dialogue with me by causing a vocational earthquake all these years later.

The tremors of my inner world continued. The pull to explore becoming some type of spiritual "something" that I had no name for became stronger. Amid my angst, I decided to talk back.

"Ok, God. If you want me to go and do this 'thing' then obviously I'm going to have to go to seminary." My statement was met with an immediate feeling of "No" and a knowing that I was to learn directly from people who were serving, loving, and leading in ways that I wanted to emulate and that I wasn't to go about obtaining a piece of paper that could give the impression that I was accessing something that wasn't readily available for all. I would have to trust that I would find my teachers and they would find me.

I now realize that my initial thoughts around going to seminary came from a place of seeking outside validation to do work I knew God was calling me to do internally. Who would take me seriously without a postgraduate degree? This is not to say that I don't value seminary or honor the path of those who have chosen to go that route. What I am saying is that for me living out the Gospels has to be accessible. It felt like a directive and an agreement in my case. Sometimes the obtaining of degrees, Ph.D.s, and mastery of subject matter connected to spirit can lull the mystic within to sleep. The sense that I was to follow a non-conventional path when it came to education and ministry continued to reveal itself. To better understand how that came to be it might be helpful to know that before the intense unraveling that was taking place, there was a breaking three years prior.

A broken relationship and broken heart partnered with the occupational crisis led me to discover the spiritual practices that would grow me into a space of trust where I felt called to serve. The fusion of it all transformed both my inner and outer worlds.

The breaking came when I was nearly eight months pregnant and learned of my partner's infidelity. This news, coupled with an already persistent yearning to discover a deeper sense of meaning and purpose in life, felt like the catalyst for impending collapse. The month I was to bring new life into the world was the month my world began falling apart.

The relationship ended, my newborn eventually became a toddler, and the frustration around discovering what I was here to do intensified with each trip into downtown Houston for my 9-to-5.

On my way home from work one evening, out of pure desperation, I pulled off the road and into a parking lot. I placed both hands on the steering wheel; my head soon followed before the familiar prayer of my teenage years found its way out of my mouth with the hope that God was listening, "I can't do this anymore. Help me."

It is difficult to describe what happened next. Somewhere within that prayer for help, there was a gentle communication back to me encouraging me to read the Bible. It wasn't audible, more like a feeling. Confused and convinced I trusted the guidance and for one year I tucked my toddler in each night, sat by her bedside and as she drifted off I read the Bible passage by passage until there were no passages left. Certain lines spoke louder to me than others, much of it I didn't understand. My life had drastically changed by the end of that year. I was left with a deep curiosity to know what was going on within the context of each biblical story. Why were these 66 books the ones that came to be known as the Bible?

Knowing what I know now about the contemplative journey I can recognize how I was unknowingly engaging in a daily practice of Lectio Divina through these nightly readings. Lectio Divina (Latin, for Divine Reading) isn't so much about how we intellectually process the words on a page, it's more about letting ourselves be read. A way of gradually growing from acquaintanceship to friendship with God. Contemplative Outreach describes it this way, "During Lectio Divina, the practitioner listens to the text of the Bible with the "ear of the heart," as if he or she is in conversation with God, and God is suggesting the topics for discussion." Yes, a relationship had fallen apart but a new one was developing; one that would lead me into the depths of the stillness, silence, and solitude of Centering Prayer. A full year with all of those words on those pages coupled with my curiosity and eventually I found myself on a retreat in the Hill Country of Texas. It is here that I met one of my first teachers on the contemplative path.

The retreat opened with a welcome and an overview of how we would spend the extended weekend together. Just before we were about to adjourn for the first evening a tall, slender gentleman with white hair was introduced. He approached the microphone slowly. He stood there, silent, and in that silence, I noticed how noisy things were within me. My mind was racing, my thoughts were loud and they began to intensify as he stood there not saying a word in front of the technology designed to carry his voice to our ears. When he did speak I listened with a certain attentiveness. His presence, his cadence, and his continued comfort with silence despite being in front of a group ready to hear him speak drew me in. He extended a general invitation to the intimate crowd to join him for a "sit" the following morning. I decided at that moment that I would accept his invitation. That "sit" served as my first official introduction to Centering Prayer back in 2015.

Centering Prayer is a form of receptive meditation that incorporates silence as a way of listening, solitude as a path to presence, and stillness as a way to discern action. Just as Lectio Divina helps to cultivate a friendship with God; Centering Prayer deepens that friendship to a place that is beyond words to communion. Yes, my world had fallen apart but a new one was emerging.

When I returned home I did my best to weave periods of Centering Prayer into my daily routine. I found early morning attempts only gave way to my exhaustion and I often drifted back to sleep. Evenings were not ideal as my toddler was now a very active 4-year-old. My practice ultimately took root within the vestibule of my Nissan Altima on my lunch breaks from doing work I no longer felt was mine to do.

Thankfully what was growing within me was not limited to the confines of my vehicle. The spiritual community I had landed in as I was searching for a place where I could ask questions about matters of life, spirit and the commingling of the two played witness to my curiosity and I was invited to start a Centering Prayer group which I was happy and excited to begin. The practice expanded from my car to one of the free rooms offered within the public library. Three attendees may have been the attendance record during that time which was a blessing considering I had no idea what I was doing.

I had no way of knowing as I sat by my daughter's bedside all those years ago feeling so alone - that the gift of Centering Prayer and a more comprehensive understanding of the contemplative journey would serve as a way that I can be present to the collective disparities magnified on a macro level in our society. In this presence, I have gained the ability to recognize and share how the contemplative mind can also serve as the creative mind that liberates and unifies so much of what is separating and dividing the world today.

My days look much different now than they did all those years ago and my expectancy has shifted. I lean heavily toward the knowing that the minutes I spend in Centering Prayer each day deeply impact all the other minutes within a 24-hour window. As a minority, a parent, and a pastor I find myself in a constant place of mystery, frustration, curiosity, and imaginative opportunity. I'm determined to illuminate ways the contemplative mind and heart can serve as a disruption to the injustices we are witnessing and experiencing today on a collective level as part of the expectation I carry for a more compassionate and just world available to us all at this moment.

My formation as pastor and contemplative teacher did not occur within the institutional settings that many, including myself, assumed it would. It transpired through periods of desperation and desolation. It revealed itself in tugs and pushes. It happened while sitting in the silence of a great hall and the proverbial dessert of the front seat of a 1998 Nissan. It emerged in a public library and within a community willing to create space for the lady who liked to sit in silence.

American author, philosopher, theologian, mystic, educator, and civil rights leader, Howard Thurman said, "You are the only you that has ever lived; your idiom is the only idiom of its kind in all of existence and if you cannot hear the sound of the genuine in you, you will all of your life spend your days on the ends of strings that somebody else pulls..."

The only strings we are here to be pulled by are those of Spirit. The mystic is aware of this and the delicate manner in which all strings are connected.

The contemplative creative mind has helped me with divisions and disparities by creating a path of connection. In gaining a glimpse into the ways I have lived divided within myself I also come to recognize how we live divided among each other. In recognizing my tendency to over-identify with the ego I recognize the illusions influencing organizations, communities, politics, and the world at large. In perceiving the influence of those illusions I discover I can ground myself in a freedom that is beyond circumstances and conditions. In grounding myself in a freedom beyond circumstance and conditions I discover the creative power we have in giving birth to a new world. One where all are welcome to the table and the illusion of any strings other than the thread of Love begins to fall away.

3

TOWARD CONTEMPLATIVE ACTION
Benjamin Perry

SNOW DRIFTS LISTLESSLY IN my sleepy Maine town. In Gaza, bombs are falling. And I sit to write the chapter on Christian mysticism I've been delaying, stretched through time and space. I moved to Maine after living in New York City for a decade because I wanted quiet, but I wasn't prepared for how stillness would disquiet my soul.

You get used to living at the beating heart, the pulse of the world's latest crisis or climax reverberates—walking before you and following behind. When death rides upon the newswire, you can taste it on the air. Living within that sounding chamber is a particular kind of attunement: In moments of acute suffering, the thrum lends an illusory connection that reminds us of our genuine interconnectedness.

I traded electricity for a vacuum, great cavernous woods that swallow sound before perception—whose emptiness seems to draw forth yearning like a paper towel pulls a spill into waiting capillaries. That wistfulness is its own potential energy, but on days like this one when my heart is breaking it can feel ominous, ready to burst.

I don't mean to make Maine—or any rural area—sound like some kind of refuge from place and time, an ontologically different category of being. Lord knows we get enough of that from the news: What do the Real American Voters think? Nor are my friends here disconnected from the world. When I bring up the war, they have thoughts; they have grief. They, too, are reading Al Jazeera. They see the craters where there once were playgrounds. But there is a relentlessness to New York that they do not share.

Somewhere in the evolution of how social media poisoned our brains, we became convinced the depths of our compassion are measured by how much we ruminate on how evil afflicts the world. Are you only thinking about the dead children for an hour each day? How could you be so calloused and unfeeling? Obviously, most people would not phrase this link so bluntly, but its truth is present in our doom scrolling. When we feel impotent to end horror, bathing our brains in violent images can provide psychic reassurance: At least I'm doing *something*. Of course, we know that incessant rumination does not make victims any safer, but it's a place for sorrow to burrow.

And yet, this recurrent cycle is also deeply linked to the capitalism that drives a city to never sleep—models that talk about "unending growth" as if that were something to be pursued, the merchants who cannibalize our attention, sell our anguish to advertisers. The average person spends almost 3 hours on social media each day. It's hard to hear God through that much noise.

When I think about mysticism, the first person who enters my mind is Thomas Merton. Merton, if you're unfamiliar, was a Trappist monk, writer and poet who, after graduating from Columbia University, lived most of his life at the Abbey of Gethsemani in rural Kentucky. (And, if you are familiar, please put this essay down and read one of his books immediately.) Throughout his life, Merton became known for his ascetic lifestyle, the profundity of his work, and his engagement with contemporary American political life. (He was, for example, a regular pen pal with President John F. Kennedy.) The fascination with Merton stems from the friction—and seeming contradiction—between these two faces of his life; his reclusion from and simultaneous interaction with the world.

Surely, part of why he jumps to mind when considering mysticism is his conformity to our platonic ideal of a mystic. While there have been many mystics who live in cities; mystics who are wild and exuberant in their demeanor; mystics who revel in worldly pleasure; I think many of us still carry notions that the *true* mystic lives a quiet life far from the tumult of modern society. But truly, the reason he occupies that dais in my thinking is the quality of his writing—the mix of quietude and crackling energy that feels, to me, the marker of living at the tangent point of God; where the divine brushes against our everyday sensibilities.

Merton's book *Raids on the Unspeakable* opens with an essay "Rain and the Rhinoceros," that exemplifies his ability to turn the mundane into a holy encounter. "The rain I am in is not like the rain of cities. It fills the woods with an immense and confused sound. It covers the flat roof of the cabin and its porch with insistent and controlled rhythms," Merton writes, "And I listen, because it reminds me again and again that the whole world runs by rhythms I have not yet learned to recognize, rhythms that are not those of the engineer."

Sitting alone in his hermitage, Merton transforms the act of sitting and listening to drops of rain into symphonic union with the Creator—relationship birthed through transforming passive observation into something akin to worship. "[The rain says] we still carry this burden of illusion because we do not dare to lay it down," he writes, "We suffer all the needs that society demands we suffer, because if we do not have these needs we lose our 'usefulness' in society…we fear to be alone, and to be ourselves, and so to remind others of the truth that is in them." That's an awful lot of meaning to be discerned in drops of rain.

In our hearts, most of us yearn for this kind of spirituality—one that can alchemically render even an experience with weather into communion. We catch glimpses on our lives' margins of how that heightened consciousness might feel, like the fleeting moment between sleeping and waking; liminal drift between one world and the next. Or when sun catches ice floating on the water at just the right angle, and it feels as if that blinding radiance might originate from within ourselves, as well. Then, the magic passes and we find ourselves returned to the quotidian realm, the Ordinary Time between transient ecstasy.

·••••••••·

THE FEAR, IT SEEMS, is that any attempt to remain in this altered state abandons our responsibility to the *real* world—the one marked by commerce and matters of space. It's all well and good for Thomas Merton to sit and find oceanic connection with the rain—he's a monk, sworn to a path outside commitment to jobs, family, and the countless pressures of daily living. And this is true! Most of us would find it impossible to dedicate the same amount of time to quiet and contemplation. That doesn't mean, however, that we can't carve *more* room in our lives for this kind of intentional relationship with the kind of slowness that makes space for the holy.

Abraham Joshua Heschel's reflection on the sabbath feels relevant, here. In his seminal work on the topic, Heschel describes Sabbath as "a palace we build in time." Humanity, he notes, is obsessed with matters of space, a focus on the immediate and material that forms the chronological axis on which we live. God's interaction with humans operates on a different plane—one which intersects this everyday existence but does not run in parallel beside it. These brief holy glimpses inspire our yearning for a deeper reverence, but we cannot truly enter that holy court without honoring its demands. "How else can we express glory in the presence of eternity, if not by the silence of abstaining from noisy acts?" he asks, "These restrictions utter songs to those who know how to stay at a palace with a queen."

Crucially, Heschel does not see withholding from everydayness as a burden, but an invitation to experience the fullness of life. It's a conviction he took to the very end of his own. In a spiritual anthology of his work compiled by his friend Rabbi Samuel H. Dresner, Dresner begins his introduction by recalling a conversation he had with Heschel at the end of his life, shortly after a debilitating heart attack. "When I regained consciousness," Heschel told his friend, "my first feelings were not of despair or anger. I felt only gratitude to God for my life, for every moment I had lived." Remembering the words he spoke to God in that moment of vulnerable fragility, Heschel shared them with his friend: "I did not ask for success; I asked for wonder. And You gave it to me."

In this exchange, we glimpse a crucial dimension of what it means to live a contemplative life. Even more than mysticism asks us to shift our daily rhythms, it demands a change in disposition. Gratitude, even in the midst of hardship, is an essential part of building that palace in which we can meet God. And there is an intimate relationship between finding quiet and nurturing that spirit. However, once we deepen our ability to sink into gratefulness it becomes a resource we can draw upon in the hustle of modern existence. And, like a river suddenly reversing its course, we also find that changing our disposition helps us find moments of solace even when we don't live deep within the Kentucky wilderness. Through mindfulness, we can all move closer to the kinds of stillness in which holiness grows.

·······

THERE'S ANOTHER CONCERN, THOUGH, that I suspect motivates personal aversion to mysticism more than simple time constraints: The conviction that, in a world bereft by so much suffering, mysticism is inescapably selfish, focused on our own experience to the detriment of society. And it's painfully true that some forms of personal spirituality do exchange relationship with the world for relationship with the self. But that is not an unavoidable destiny; it's a function of how capitalism has cheapened and commoditized our picture of mystical life.

Turning again to Merton's work, we see spirituality deeply concerned with the world outside his hermitage. In his essay "Letter to an Innocent Bystander," found in the same volume that begins with his reflection on the rain, Merton is deeply troubled by confusing quiet for passivity. "Unless our waiting implies knowledge and action, we will find ourselves waiting for our own destruction and nothing more," he writes, "A witness of a crime, who just stands by and makes a mental note of the fact that he is an innocent bystander, tends by that very fact to become an accomplice."

Merton was vocal in his support for the Civil Rights movement well before it became mainstream and while many of his white contemporaries condemned it. As a Columbia student, he regularly volunteered with the Friendship House in Harlem, folding clothes and taking on other decidedly unglamorous tasks that needed doing. Later in his life, he became passionate about building inter-religious relationships, setting to this work with such intention that the Dalai Lama once praised him as having a deeper understanding of Buddhism than any other Christian. He regularly used his position and platform to draw attention to the hour's most pressing crises. But throughout, his activism was always tethered to contemplative practice that carefully considered each choice.

That intention is something I think many of us would do well to learn from in this era that often prioritizes the quantity of one's words and actions over their quality. In a letter Merton wrote to Jim Forest—then a young organizer working to end the war in Vietnam—he cautioned Forest, "It is so easy to get engrossed with ideas and slogans and myths that in the end one is left holding the bag, empty, with no trace of meaning left in it."

The forces that attempt to commodify resistance have only increased in sophistication and scope in the decades since Merton wrote those words. Social media, in particular, has become an arena where people feel compelled to signify their alignment with just causes, often before they have done the work to truly understand them. One of the profoundly frustrating experiences in recent months has been watching people post about the genocide in Gaza, saying things whose core convictions I support but phrased in ways that intensify binary thinking and radicalism that fuels the ongoing violence. (For example, spreading misinformation, aligning with antisemitic tropes, or suggesting the expulsion of Israelis as the only solution to this horror.) I know these statements come from a place of empathy and hurt, the product of watching relentless atrocity. But that does not absolve their impact, which collectively contributes to making Palestinians less safe.

Many folks who are posting had never read about the history of Palestine before October 7th and are now simultaneously: learning in real-time, processing their emotions while watching genocide unfold, and trying to add something distinctive to the cultural conversation. That is not a recipe for wisdom. Ultimately, blame does not lie with the individual—we have been told, again and again, silence is complicity. Unfortunately, the people who benefit most from that simplistic equation are those who profit from our relentlessly using social media. Sometimes, silence is the fertile soil where deeper understanding grows.

Half a century after Merton, another mystic who traded life in the city for the rolling Kentucky hills. Formed and shaped in rural life, bell hooks balanced fierce social criticism with careful contemplation. In her book *Love As the Practice of Freedom,* she speaks to the necessity of holistic understanding as a foundation to social action. "Acknowledging the truth of our reality, both individual and collective, is a necessary stage for personal and political growth," she writes, "This is usually the most painful stage in the process of learning to love." Part of that pain comes from the need to read, study and pray—to engage in careful self-work—when it is easier and often feels pressing to act and speak.

In her book *All About Love,* she expands on this essential truth in an entire chapter dedicated to the kinds of love we must nurture within ourselves so we can engage with worldly justice while minimizing unintended consequences—collateral damage rippling outward from pain we have not processed, or ignorance we have not illuminated. "The more we accept ourselves, the better prepared we are to take responsibility in all areas of our lives," she writes, "simply taking responsibility does not mean that we can prevent discriminatory acts from happening... [but affirms] the capacity to invent our lives, to shape our destinies in ways that maximize well-being. Every day. We practice this shape shifting to cope with realities we cannot easily change."

In the quiet where we meet God, we are given the opportunity to reflect on the ways we have acted, their alignment or misalignment with our deepest values. We can affirm our basic goodness, even when have made mistakes or caused harm to another person. And we give ourselves room to grow in fluid reciprocity with a God who is becoming.

This stillness is not useful to capitalism. It generates no ad revenue, garners no followers, receives no likes or shares. But it is indispensable to a moral life—we cannot flourish while only living in the spotlight. The demand to perform every aspect of our lives is an impediment to purposeful living.

···•·•••··

THERE'S A LITTLE GAME I play with my fireplace. Our primary source of heat is a Russian masonry heater—a remarkable device that uses twisting tunnels of brick to distribute warmth throughout the home. One of the amazing aspects of this system is the ability to finely control airflow, making the fire burn more or less intensely. At night, before I go to bed, I load the firebox with wood and close the vents, letting embers gently smolder in the night. And usually, when I wake in the morning, there are still one or two remaining. The game, then, is to try to use those tiny sparks to ignite the next day's fire without any matches.

The *reason* I do this—beyond whimsy in the long dark months—is that, day after day, the seamless connection between yesterday's embers and the fresh morning's blaze creates a sense of continuity—a ritual by which I am reminded how all life is interconnected, the interplay between what has passed and what is coming. It's also a visceral manifestation of hope, to see how even the smallest spark can—through breath and coaxing—create something that will warm me all day long.

And there is an integral relationship between this quiet ritualized hope and my broader hope for the world; the strength I am able to muster for action. Quiet moments where I see God help to fight the nihilism that otherwise threatens to consume my vision, whispering lies about inevitable decline. By attuning my heart to soft resilience, I reject the voice who asks, "Why bother?" If that little ember can start a fire, my actions—however ill-matched they feel to the magnitude of our problems—can spark broader change.

This productive friction between stillness and action nurtures both ends of that spectrum. Contemplative relationship with God helps guide the work of our hands, encouraging us to think deeply about *what* we are doing and *how* we are doing it. Commitment to activism ensures that stillness does not tumble into navel-gazing, remaining engaged with the broader world. To play off Dr. King's thoughts on love and power: Without quiet, action becomes scattered and frenetic; without action, quiet becomes empty and solipsistic. The mystical life is filled with both.

4

THE SUBVERSTIVE PATH OF THE MYSTIC

Brandan Robertson

AT THE CORE OF virtually every spiritual tradition throughout human history are "the mystics." The mystics are those in each tradition who are committed to the core transformative truth at the heart of all true religion- that *love* is the way, the truth, and the life- and resist the human propensity to institutionalize and dogmatize this core truth into a religious or political system which inevitably leads to burying this truth beneath orthodoxies, rituals, and rules that do very little to actually connect us to the transformative power of love. The mystics are those who are committed to the simple way, the basic principles, mindsets, and practices that help humans become more loving, and thus, more like God whose fundamental nature is love.

But as mystics remain persistent in the truth that love is the way, they are often brought into direct conflict with the powers that be- religious, social, and political- who have a vested interest in the upkeep of the institutions and systems that have been built on the foundation of this truth but no longer reflect this truth in the ways that they function. Human systems and institutions inevitably become bent towards privileging certain groups of people and excluding and oppressing others. They often begin using fear as a tactic to manipulate people into submitting to their authority, which they often claim as "divine." And when these sorts of systems and institutions fully mature, they become destructive not only to those who adhere to them but to everyone around them. This couldn't be further from the way of love.

In light of these realities, mystics spend much of their time remaining persistent in teaching the simple way of love, a way that calls us to seek inner peace and justice and then to move outwards to establish the same peace and justice in the world around us. But peace and justice often means shining a light on the fear-based divisions and injustices of the very institutions that claim to be the stewards of the spiritual tradition the mystics are a part of. This, of course, does not make the mystic very popular. In fact, in virtually all religious traditions, mystics become increasingly demonized as heretics and false teachers, stoking fear in the hearts of the faithful who would otherwise be drawn towards the truth of the mystic, and prevents true spiritual transformation and reformation from occurring in a religious, political, or cultural system.

But this does not stop the mystics. On the margins of religion, culture, and society, they continue to speak the truth, practice the simple way, and their persistence draws people, slowly but surely, to a realization of the truth. People begin to see that the mystics often look and sound a lot more like the founders of their religion—Jesus or Buddha for instance—and they begin to realize that the religious, political, and cultural systems that they have been a part of have very little to do with the core spiritual truths that can bring about true transformation. This, understandably, causes anger and resentment for many people who feel duped into wasting their lives to be a part of a system that was never interested in true personal or social transformation, but exploitation. And this fire of frustration often leads to reformation and revolution.

This is the prophetic power of the mystic- without spending a great deal of time directly critiquing their religious and political systems, their steadfast commitment to embodying the simple way of love exposes the spiritual and moral rot at the heart of many systems and institutions. Their lives show us what is possible when we simply learn to love God, love our neighbors, and love ourselves with our full hearts, often apart from the complex doctrines, dogmas, and rituals that our traditions demand that we adhere to. Inner transformation and social renewal are not as complex or as scary as we were taught—it takes place through regular rhythms of love, embodied every day. One doesn't need a priest or a president to transform the world—each one of us have the full power and potential to do that on our own, and infinitely more power when we come together in communal rhythms of love.

But this realization poses a major problem for our religious, cultural, and political systems—without our faithful obedience to the myth of their divine authority, they have no power or influence. And without power and influence, those who have risen through the ranks of the system and who've gained privilege through perpetuating the system are exposed as imposters. Many such people do not *believe* they're imposters—they may not even consciously realize that they have been a part of an oppressive institution. Many who lead religious and political institutions are true believers—after all, the system seems to have worked for them, just look at who they've become!

What they fail to realize is that for the vast majority of others who are a part of their institution, the path to their exaltation has brought profound fear, anxiety, and a loss of a sense of their true selves. Yet even the lay people struggle to see this as a bad thing—after all, if God has demanded that they be fearful, that they repress themselves, that they pour out their lives to keep an institution growing strong, what could be more righteous? This sense of fear-based righteousness, even at great cost to their own flourishing, keeps people locked into their religious and political institutions. And even as some may have inklings that all is not right, the shame that comes from admitting that they've devoted their lives to an illegitimate path and the fear of losing whatever community and status they have gained in that tradition makes critiquing or leaving an implausible option. So often, they double down.

Yet even in the face of this reality, mystics remain persistent, and their work and witness continue to beckon those within the religious tradition to *"taste and see"* (Psalm 34:8) that there is a better way. The mystics' life and teachings stand as an oasis in the spiritual desert of our religious and political traditions, enticing the faithful to remember that there is *true* spiritual nourishment available to them that is *free*. As the Prophet Isaiah wrote, *"Come, all you who are thirsty, come to the waters; and you who have no money, come, buy and eat! Come buy wine and milk without money and without cost!"* (Isaiah 55:1) Yet for so many of us, conditioned by the belief that spiritual transformation *must be costly and burdensome* resist this invitation, thinking that it's a watered-down, hedonistic, libertine knock-off of "true faith." How could it truly be that simple?

But this is the prophetic message of the mystic: it *is* that simple. It *is* that easy. The path to spiritual and social liberation can *only* come from humanity waking up to the love of God, love of neighbor, and love of self. As the mystic Jesus said, all other religious and social laws and prophetic writings are summed up in these three directives. (Matthew 22:40) The *only* practices that we *need* are those that provoke us towards love. The *only* creed we need to believe in is that *love is the way*. There is no other way, no other truth, no other path to abundant life. This is it. And it's not a Christian message or a Jewish message or a

Buddhist message or a Muslim message—it's the message that is at the core of every single one of the world's religious traditions. It's the aim of every legitimate political movement. It's the singular desire at the core of every single person—to love, to be loved, and to know love.

The thing about love is that it cannot be institutionalized or systematized. You cannot believe your way to or ritualize love. Love cannot be attained through performance. Love will not be withheld by our flaws or failures. Love is not a reward that we gain through faithful obedience but is the core of our reality. Love does not require a meditator to access it- it is free to everyone at every moment. And when we experience the power of love, it provokes us to express it, to share it, to make its presence known in the world. This is why every legitimate mystic is not merely a monk in a cave, cut off from the world, but those who are committed to tangible acts of charity and justice in their world. Love doesn't drive us away from the world, but deeper into it. Love invites us into a rhythm of inward contemplation and outward action. Love expels our fear, making us brave in the face of scrutiny and hated, because we realize that nothing and no one can diminish our belovedness, and we begin to see even our enemies as those who deserve our love.

Because of this, mystics transform their world. Think of some of the most well-known mystics of our modern age: Thomas Merton, Dorothy Day, Desmond Tutu, the Dalai Lama, Martin Luther King Jr, Abraham Joshua Heschel, Mahatma Ghandi, Mother Theresa, Maya Angelou, Richard Rohr, Thich Nhat Hanh—all these individuals were beacons not merely of inner transformation but social transformation. Every single one of these people were marginalized by the religious establishments of their day, yet their witness to the simple way of love shone so brightly that not even the worst critique or persecution could dim their light. Billions of people were drawn towards the truth that they embodied, and experienced profound social and spiritual transformation. This is the power of the mystic—their words and witness always find a way to make it to the people who need it the most, even as institutions try to silence and demonize them. Mystics often aren't *trying* to infiltrate their religious systems, but the nature of truth is that it will always proceed forth and "will never return void." (Isaiah 55:11) Just by embodying the truth of love in their lives, they ignite transformation and renewal.

This is a far more important characteristic of a mystic than many realize—many people have been hurt or at very least disillusioned by religious systems and often act out of that pain in an attempt to dismantle the corrupt systems that have caused them harm. This is an understandable reaction, and the impulse to expose corrupt systems and leaders is a just one. But the truth is that when we're acting from unhealed wounds, we lack clarity and precision in our critique. When we try to offer an alternative to the religious paths that have hurt us while we're still bleeding, it is far too easy for us to fall into unhealthy and unhelpful patterns ourselves. Many mystics have started their journeys through facing religious rejection, but before they discover the transformative power of love or immediately beginning to try to offer an alternative path, they do the work to heal their wounds, to understand the systems that they've escaped from, and are then moved by compassion rather than acute pain to speak prophetic truths that begin to chip away at the foundations of unjust religious systems. Anger has a place in the path of the mystic- it must be experienced, walked through, and accepted as legitimate. But it should not be allowed to stagnate—to stop us on the journey of spiritual renewal but should move us towards healing. As Lama Rod Owens said, "*We must allow the anger to be in our experience... And that if we don't wrestle with anger, we will never get to the heartbreak. And if we don't get to the heartbreak, we don't get to the healing."*[1]

The mystic is one who makes space to process their just anger, to uncover the heartbreak it reveals, and to meet that heartbreak with the power of love which can bring healing to their soul and fuel to their journey to forge a new path. Instead of merely tearing down that which is corrupt, the mystic is one who seeks to build up those which fuels the evolution of their soul and world. Dorothy Day founded the Catholic Worker House, Martin Luther King Jr. launched the Civil Rights Movement, and Father Richard Rohr built the Center for Action and Contemplation. Love *always* builds up—it doesn't only invite us to a new way of feeling but provokes us to actually *manifest* love in our world in tangible ways. True spiritual transformation will *always* result in inward and *outward* transformation. This is a telltale sign of those who are truly walking the mystic's path and those who are trying to capitalize on the idea of being a "mystic."

The mystic is one who has come to see that the subversion of unjust and stagnant religion comes through a radical, persistent commitment to love. They do the work to grow in their awareness that love is all there is and that they are loved and love at their core. They do the work to share this experience and truth with others. And they do the work to make this truth not merely an inner experience but a tangible reality in the world around them. And through this simple path, they ignite vast movements of transformation.

HOW TO WALK THE MYSTIC PATH

The inevitable question that you may be asking is *how* one can actually *become* a mystic. If you're reading this book, I assume you're already on your way. If you resonate with the description of the mystics path above, then you're likely on the threshold of your own mystical journey. But here's the thing—one doesn't become a mystic by choosing to. Rather, the transformation into what we call a "mystic" comes gradually through practicing love with persistence. It's rather off putting when an individual makes the claim that they are mystic, isn't it? Even as I write this chapter, I would not presume to call myself a "mystic." I am aiming at the mystic's path, and I am seeking to walk the simple way of love in my life, but what I've recognized both in my study of the mystics and the profound opportunities I have had to be mentored by many modern day mystics is that the transformation into a truly mystical life happens gradually and often unexpectedly. This is the frustrating truth about the spiritual life- one cannot simply take a course to become enlightened. It takes lived experiences, mistakes, and a persistent commitment to love in order to be refined and re-formed into a truly mystical life. We can *desire* the mystics path and can learn from those who have become considered to be mystics, but just agreeing with or even engaging in their practices doesn't automatically *make* us a mystics. *Life* is what makes us a mystic. Walking through this world, step by step, aiming to see and to be love is what refines our soul and calibrates our heart to the energy of the divine, and the more we pursue this path, the more likely it is that one day we may find ourselves being called "mystics" by others.

Some may not agree with my assessment here. After all, the dictionary definition of mystic is "*a person who seeks by contemplation and self-surrender to obtain unity with or absorption into the Deity or the absolute*"- if you're *seeking* to be united with the divine, then by this definition you are a mystic. That's *all of us* who have written and all of you who are reading this book. But what most of us tend to mean when we call someone a mystic is one who has *attained* a sense of surrender or unity with love. That is what we are ultimately aiming to become. But it seems to me that seeking to claim the title of "mystic" is often just another way for our ego to give ourselves some of the authority or status that we gave up when we left our institutional religion behind. The mystic journey is not about *being labeled a mystic*, but about living mystically until we are transformed in mind, body and spirit. By seeking a title or a status, we actually can derail our journey, becoming just as arrogant and self-righteous as other religious fundamentalists. They mystic's journey is one of humility, its one of being and becoming, not about *arriving* at some grand finish line.

Our job as those seeking to walk the mystics path is unglamorous and frustratingly simple- it does not require that we take a year to travel to far off lands on pilgrimage or go on psychedelic journeys. (Though both things *can* be helpful aids on the journey) But if we truly want to experience the world as mystics, we must ground ourselves in the simple path of love- loving God, loving our neighbors and the world around us, and loving ourselves. We must resist beliefs that cause us to be afraid of or demonize others. We must resist the egoic urge for certainty and answers. We must be convinced of only one truth- that love is all that there is and love is all that matters. In every circumstance, when we choose to see and act in love, the eyes of our soul will gradually open and we will begin to perceive the deepest truth of reality- in love we live, move, and have our being. Love is all and in all- even when it's hard to see. Our job is to speak love in the face of fear and injustice, to act in love in the face of anger and division, and to know deep in our bones that we are *beloved* and see everyone and everything as beloved as well. Then, and only then, will we be transformed into mystics.

---

1. Lama Rod Owens, *Love and Rage: The Path of Liberation Through Anger*, xiv.

5
RUNNING BETWEEN WORDS AND WORLDS
Carl Amouzou

"Be present in all things ...."

— Maya Angelou

•••••••••

YOU ARE LOVED.

You are forgiven.

You belong here.

These three statements were the beginning of my contemplative journey. I would wake up in the morning and recite these phrases to myself while looking in the mirror. When I had to go somewhere that caused me to be anxious, I would place my right hand over my heart and repeat those words. These were words that I felt that God had spoken to me at a really low place in my life when all three of those phrases were things I could not believe. But as Abraham Joshua Heschel says, "Words create worlds." And I wished to build my reality upon these words.

For a long time, I would say these words to myself at least once a day. These words were healing. These words were restorative. But as one tends to do over time, I forgot about the words that had begun to create my world.

About a year ago, I was sitting with my therapist working through grief and loss. My sister had recently passed away from an aggressive form of cancer. I was sharing that out of all the things I was feeling the strongest was anger. I conveyed how I am not allowed to convey anger in this world. He asked me "What do you think would happen if you allowed yourself to not just feel anger but display it?" I looked down, then back up at him, and said, "I would probably get arrested or killed by the police. Nothing is scarier in white society than the angry black man." My therapist, who was a middle-aged white man stopped, began to fumble over his words, and then eventually apologized for not being able to understand my experience.

Facing myself in this moment of counseling, I bore witness to how I have internalized a narrative that said I am too much, what I feel will not be accepted by others, and even worse it could cause others to harm me. This narrative asked me to take up less space. It called me to become more disembodied. This narrative whispered to me you are unloved; you do not belong here.

Every year, I take the first two weeks to pray and listen; pray about what this next year will bring; Listening for a word that will epitomize the coming year, a theme of sorts. Last year, the word was Liberation. I am always surprised by how these words show up in my life. Over the next year, I learned how liberation would show up in my life. I was going to be liberated from the stories I had been telling myself, the stories others had told me were mine, and the stories that society had constructed to box me in. Nothing is more powerful than the stories we come to believe. They create the materials from which we build our realities; my reality had begun to collapse in on itself.

There are moments in our lives that reveal to us that we are living in a false reality. These moments betray the comfort of the simulation. They show us that the constructed reality is obscuring the truth of our lives. In other words, the stories that we have allowed to create our world might be hiding the potential and possibility of the world we are meant to live in.

In my case, I was not meant to live in an ever-shrinking world that did not have space for me. Instead, I am meant to live in a world that is generative and generous. A world where one does not simply take up space, but rather one where space is a blessing that we give and receive in reciprocity. A world that one is joyously participating in co-creating. A world where one wholly and holy belongs. But one must be liberated to this world. I must be liberated to this world.

There is a scene in C.S. Lewis' book, The Magician's Nephew, where the main character begins to enter into new worlds through portals. Some of these worlds are places of death and some are places where new life begins. I imagine the stories we allow to create our worlds are like these portals transporting us into the realms of possibility.

What does liberation mean and look like in this context? That is the first question that I am asking myself and working through. Liberation for me looks like letting go of stories that stop me from being present to the possibility of the generative and generous world. Stories that tell me to take up as little space as possible lest I disrupt and disturb those around me. Stories that tell me I do not belong. Stories that tell me "That isn't for you Carl." As long as I am holding onto those stories, I cannot embrace stories that invite me into liberation. I am learning that the stories that I have held onto for so long were stories justifying the distance, disconnection, and disembodiment I practiced. The stories that I am now telling myself and trying to practice are all about presence.

How do you practice being present? This is the second question that I am asking. Being present has always been a hard concept for my mind and body to grasp. One of my mentors previously described me as someone who lives in the future and every once in a while visits the present. I used to hold that as high praise, Carl the Futurist. But over the past few years, I have come to see it as less of a compliment and more as a description of a detriment. Maybe it is better stated as I have begun to see it as a diagnosis of a condition that has left me far too often feeling disconnected and isolated. Living in the future was easier for me than admitting to myself that I was scared to be present. Being present meant that I had to own the space that I now stand in. Going back to the stories that I had come to believe about myself, owning the space that one stands in was not something for people like me.

Over the years I have used the language of presence without fully understanding what it meant to be present. Theoretically and conceptually I knew, but to actually allow my whole self to show up in any given moment was as foreign to me as settlers arriving on distant shores. I have always believed at some level that depending on where I am I must negotiate what part of me can show up.

Henri Nouwen says, "Hope prevents us from clinging to what we have and frees us to move away from the safe place and enter unknown and fearful territory." Hope beckoned to me to let go of the stories in my life that were holding me hostage. What I had were toxic narratives that constructed a cage. What I needed was the courage to step out onto the distant shores of a new story. I needed a way to be present with myself and to myself, and this was an unknown and fearful territory. I needed a way to move from conceptually present to embodied presence.

I had recently started running. And on this particular night, the rain was pouring as it tends to do in Vancouver BC. I set out for my run and my AirPods decided that Bluetooth was a theoretical construct that they could ignore. About a kilometer in, my headphones cut out and I was left with my own thoughts and the sound of my breath to keep me company as I finished my run. I had never noticed that the thoughts that raced through my head as I ran were a torrent of negative comments about myself.

"Keep moving you fat bastard."

"Just stop. you look ridiculous."

Were these thoughts there all along but only drowned out by the music? When I got home that night after my run, I had to sit with the revelation that running wasn't for someone like me was a story being rehearsed over and over again in my mind without me even noticing it. Had I not been forced to be present in that moment I don't know if I would have ever discovered the repeating mixtape of negativity that was playing just below my consciousness.

I should back up a little in the story. I have long admired runners, maybe the word envied would be more accurate. I have long desired to run; it always seemed like something that I would love if I could only do it. But growing up between bad knees and asthma running seemed to elude me. As an adult, I kept that narrative going and added the fact that I have been morbidly obese for much of my adult life. So running wasn't for someone like me. By happenstance, while I was scrolling through Instagram, I saw someone running and it looked like their feet were gliding instead of "pounding the pavement." After a little research, I learned that this was demonstrating proper running technique and that if done correctly running strengthened your knees instead of hurting them. This information sat in the back of my head for a couple of years, and then one night I decided to test the theory that proper technique wouldn't hurt my knees. I decided to run to the mailbox down the street and back, about half a kilometer in total. My legs burned. My lungs gasped. However, my knees were pain-free. And this was the genesis of my journey with running. A few nights a week I would put my AirPods in and head out the door listening to Stic from dead prez's "Fit-Hop" albums. I enjoyed running. It was a moment where I drowned out the world and escaped.

I tried running with a pair of old wired headphones, but I couldn't stop thinking about the thoughts my mind pushed to the surface when the headphones went quiet. I committed to running for a while without headphones, music, or distractions. I wanted to be present in my runs. I wanted to hear what my thoughts were conveying when they weren't being muted by the music in my headphones. Instead of drowning out my thoughts, I began to re-author the narrative that was playing below the surface of my conscious mind. I began to notice the way my breath would rise and fall with every step. I began to think about the way that our breath connects us to the divine and to the creation around us; we inhale the breath of God and exhale our breath only for it to be inhaled by the flora all around us. Running in this way was a form of learning to be present in a way I had never been before. Running became meditation. Running went from an enjoyable distraction to a mindful presence akin to the breath prayer.

You are loved.

You are forgiven.

You belong here.

I found myself beginning to recite these old familiar phrases once again, but now as I ran.

Inhale. You are loved. Exhale. I am loved.

Inhale. You are forgiven. Exhale. I am forgiven.

Inhale. You belong here. Exhale. I belong here.

My running became my prayer. I run for all sorts of reasons, but mostly, I find myself looking forward to that moment when I am present both to myself and with myself in the midst of creation. I am not thinking about the future. I am not thinking about the past. I am thinking about this present moment and how I am present in it in a way that I have never been before and will never be again. I may run by the same row of houses tomorrow, but who I am in this moment will not.

It was foggy out. I remember thinking that the streetlights looked like something out of a dream sequence. "I'll kill you nigger!" bellowed a voice from somewhere behind me to the right. I was suddenly brought to attention as I was snatched out of my peace. I kept running because I didn't believe my ears had heard what they heard. After another few lines threatening bodily harm, I stopped. It came from the darkness of one of three houses but I couldn't make out which one. Everything in me wanted to search for the offender, the thief of my peace. In that moment, something spoke to me, reminding me that no matter what you are loved. No matter what you are forgiven. No matter what you belong here. I turned around and continued down the street. Every time the thought of going back to confront the anonymous assailant surfaced, I found myself reciting my breath prayer. I also found myself thinking about Ahmad Aubrey, who lost his life going for a run. I found myself thinking about my ancestors who were forced to run to escape being taken. Running at that moment was no longer about being present to the peace I felt from running. It was about being present in all things. As much as I was tempted to avoid that street, I ran it the next day. I allowed my breath to be my prayer that said "I belong here."

I have run that street dozens of times since that incident. The story that the anonymous voice wanted me to believe, is that I don't belong there. What this past year has taught me is that no one has the power to believe and accept the narratives that shape my life except me. I am not going to pretend that the words that were yelled at me that night don't replay in my head every single time I run past that house. Every time those thoughts arise, my breath reminds me that I do belong.

Inspired by the short film, Every Single Street, about a runner named Rickey Gates who ran every street in San Francisco, all 1,300 plus miles, I set out to run the four square blocks around my house weekly, all roughly five kilometers of it. The purpose of this project is to take up space, know that I belong, and create a story I want to inhabit in the place I live. This run is a prayer.

Inhale. You are loved. Exhale. I am Loved.

Inhale. You are forgiven. Exhale. I am forgiven.

Inhale. You belong here. Exhale. I belong here.

Every time I go on this run through my neighborhood, these words have become generative and expansive. They have moved from being about me to being about every single person who lives within the sound of my breath. These words have become words of reciprocity.

These words are spoken to my neighbor who called the police on me for looking suspicious. These words are spoken to my neighbor whose partner just passed away and she is uncertain about her future. These words are spoken to the anonymous voice that espoused hatred in my direction. These words are spoken to my neighbors who sit on their front porch most nights and always smile and wave when I run by.

Before my headphones shorted out in the rain, I had never noticed all the things that have become so meaningful to me in my neighborhood. Before my headphones shorted out, I ran through my community the same way that I answered greetings, in the least disruptive way possible to take up as little space as possible.

I want to be present to it all. The beauty of that is that even the painful and hurtful stories can be re-articulated and re-authored into stories that create life and joy. Without the disruptive moments, I would not have found my way to the moments that write the stories I want to create my world. A world where I am loved and I love. A world where I am forgiven and I forgive. A world where I belong and I cultivate the possibility for others to belong.

When last year started, I never thought that the word, liberation, would show up in my life the way that it did. I never thought that it would show up inviting me to let go of the stories in my life that told me not to be present. I never thought that it would cause me to literally run away when confronted with a story that was counter to the one I want to shape my world. Running created the space for me to resonate with the truth of Maya Angelou's words, "Be present in all things."

I am loved. I am Forgiven. I belong here.

6
NURTURING OUR OWN INNER MYSTIC
Caroline Oakes

I RECENTLY HEARD A beautiful story about a moment of awe and wonder that Albert Einstein experienced as a little boy, about six or seven years old. I am captivated by the way physicist Brian Cox recounted the story. He said—

> ... And his dad gave [young Einstein] a compass, and so he looked at the compass and he saw that, "Well, there's this *thing*, there's this *needle*, that always points north, always points in this one direction. So there's something invisible that I can't see, that underlies our reality, that is making this needle point north."

> Later in life, Einstein said that 'it was my first encounter with an idea, which is: If you look at Nature carefully, and really pay attention, and you're lucky... you can catch a glimpse of something deeply hidden.' Which is a beautiful phrase—*something deeply hidden*... which is the deep structure of reality. It's what our reality is."

Einstein's words here—"catch a glimpse of something deeply hidden... really pay attention... look at Nature carefully"—this is the language of *mystics*.

And while Albert Einstein was one of the most accomplished scientists of our time, it is he who also said that "the most beautiful emotion we can experience is *the mystical*," one in which we are able "to wonder and to stand rapt in awe."

· · · · ● · ● · · · ·

EACH ONE OF US, at different points in our lives, has experienced such moments of awe and wonder—moments that connect us with something deeply hidden, a reality we long to catch more than a glimpse of. Might we all have within us an *inner mystic* longing for us to notice the awe and wonder that is an ever-present part of our everyday lives?

I believe we do.

AWE AND WONDER

Professor Dasher Keltner is an expert on awe and wonder. A University of California, Berkeley, professor of psychology, Dr. Keltner is the author of *Awe: The New Science of Everyday Wonder and How It Can Transform Your Life*. He, like Einstein, also assures us that "there are so many opportunities for [even] everyday awe. Awe is almost always nearby."

In the numerous studies of experiences of awe that he recounts in his book, Dr. Keltner tells us that a clear motif emerges: Our individual self gives way to the boundary-dissolving sense "of being part of something much larger."

"Awe frees us," Dr. Keltner says, "to go in search of 'the all,' a life of expanding freedom and empowerment." And awe is also easily "findable"—

> Awe is found in the wonders of life—the strength, courage, and kindness of others; collective movement and actions like dance and sports; nature; music; art and visual design; mystical encounters; encountering life and death; and big ideas or epiphanies. These wonders are all around us, if we only pause for a moment and open our minds.

If we only pause for a moment and open our minds.

This observation of Dr. Keltner's is key here, and important for us to pay attention to. After all, every world spiritual tradition has been trying to tell us this for thousands of years—that through pausing for a moment and opening our minds through contemplative practices of silence and solitude, we become more aware of ourselves, of others, and of the awe and wonder of the world around us.

And now the exciting new field of "contemplative neuroscience" is confirming the perennial truths of these very traditions—that by pausing for a moment and opening our minds in contemplative practice, when we let go of, or "surrender," our thoughts and return to our center, we are actually rewiring our brain. In our "letting go," neurons are firing together and wiring new neural pathways that give us greater access to the higher functions of our brain, enabling us to become more insightful, less overreactive, more aware of the world around us.

Indeed, Dr. Keltner's explorations of the phenomenon of awe have brought him what he calls "the conviction that awe... is a pathway to healing and growing in the face of the losses and traumas that are part of life." He says,

> How does awe transform us? By quieting the nagging, self-critical, over bearing, status–conscious voice of our self, or ego... [at the same time] awe empowers us to collaborate, to open our mind to wonders, and to see the deep patterns of life.

The words Dr. Keltner uses as an explorer of awe and wonder is *also* the language of mystics—"boundary dissolving... in search of the 'all'... being part of something larger... transcendence."

And each one of us, by our given natures, has this very capacity to stop and notice moments of awe, and in those moments to feel a connection with "something deeply hidden," transcendent, beyond thought, Holy, even—what Thomas Keating and Richard Rohr name (when speaking to multi-faith groups) as "Ultimate Reality, or God, as we call that reality in the Judeo-Christian tradition."

THE MYSTIC WITHIN

So again I wonder—might we all have within us an **inner mystic**—a part of us that longs to be seen and nurtured *by us*, that is nudging us, even prompting us, to find practices that will help us slow down, "open our minds," and more fully take in the awe and wonder that is a sometimes hidden but nonetheless ever-present part of our everyday lives, knowing that if we do, we will see with new eyes and experience a deeper connection with ourselves, with others, and with the world around us?

I believe this is so. And it makes sense to me that more of us are coming to recognize this part inside of us, this inner mystic within and its promptings toward desiring a more open and inclusive and fluid spiritual life than the one given to us as children and young adults.

Might it even be our own inner mystic within that is prompting the process that many of us find ourselves in these days—deconstructing and re-constructing our sense of Western Christianity, of institutionalized authority, of tradition, of Scripture, even, and of where we ourselves fit within our new realities?

EAST AND WEST

It wasn't until I attended seminary that I had any awareness at all that the Western Christianity in which I grew up was in any way fundamentally different from *Eastern* Christianity. Eastern Christian spirituality appeared on my spiritual landscape during a midsummer afternoon seminary class that I will never forget, and I have been drawn to its powerful, more contemplative, practices and way of being ever since.

It was there in that seminary class that I learned the entirely new (to me) *wisdom*-oriented Eastern way of understanding the Christian gospels as a mystical *path* of spiritual awakening and of inner transformation, a path that honors the inner mystic within all of us.

I found this new Eastern perspective enlightening and enlivening. I am "nerding out" here a bit... but I began to see that Christianity in the West puts a high priority on order, uniformity, and authority and is predominately savior-oriented, or *soteriological*, with its theological emphasis on being saved, redeemed from sin, and reconciled with God by Jesus.

In contrast to the West, Christianity in the Eastern part of the Christian world today (and earliest Christianity) is predominantly *sophiological*, meaning it is mostly wisdom-oriented (*sophia* being the Greek word for "wisdom"). Its theological emphasis is on pursuing a transformative wisdom path of spiritual practices that equip us to see past our ego-self, to see what seems hidden, to pay attention, to connect with the Spirit of God.

As Cynthia Bourgeault explains in her groundbreaking book *Wisdom Jesus: Transforming Heart and Mind—A New Perspective on Christ and His Message*, "A *sophiological* Christianity focuses on the path. It emphasizes how Jesus is like us, how what he did in himself is what we are called to do in ourselves."

Through the recent work of Richard Rohr, Cynthia Bourgeault, the late Thomas Keating, and other teachers of Christian contemplative practice and the wisdom tradition, a growing number of Western Christians are now shifting a bit eastward, toward this more Eastern Christian wisdom orientation. With less focus on doctrinal systems and on what constitutes *"belief"* in Jesus, the emphasis of this wisdom movement is on experiencing the *awakened way of being* that Jesus embodied, particularly in the context of Jesus' own profound contemplative awareness practice and his central message for us to... "see beyond our minds."

METANOIA

Of critical importance in this ancient/new Eastern orientation that is capturing the minds of many in the Christian West is the increased awareness of the mistranslation of the word "repent" from its original Greek word "*metanoia*" in the Christian New Testament. Some describe this mistranslation as tragic; others describe it as the worst translation in the entire New Testament![1] This is because, in their opinion, the true meaning of *metanoia* actually conveys the very *essence* of the Christian gospel and the central message of Jesus' ministry.

The Rev. David Anderson, author of the book *Losing Your Faith, Finding Your Soul: The Passage to New Life When Old Beliefs Die,* explained the details around this mistranslation beautifully in his weekly online *Finding Your Soul* blog. He says,

> The original word for *repent* is not so much lost, as destroyed in translation. Wherever in the New Testament we see the word "repent," it's a gross mistranslation of *metanoia*.

> The problem seems to have begun with Jerome, who in 382 translated the Greek New Testament into the Latin *Vulgate*. When Jerome got to Matthew 3 and the advent of John the Baptist, he read "*Metanoia*, for the kingdom of heaven is at hand." Jerome rendered the Greek *metanoia* as, "Do penance." Thereafter, that translation was picked up in countless Bibles—"*Repent,* for the kingdom of heaven is at hand."

Metanoia now meant doing penance, and from there it was a short leap to self-flagellation, thumbs screws and hairshirts. All of that was eventually swept into the trash-can of bad theology, but the word lived on. It still meant self-condemnation, guilt and renunciation of sin.

Yet when John the Baptist and Jesus used the word, they meant something remarkable. *Meta* (after or beyond) + *noia* (mind) means literally "going beyond your mind." It's shifting into a new mindset, sloughing off your old state of mind and seeing the world from a new vantage point. It's exactly what Paul means when he urges his readers to undergo a transplant and take on the "mind of Christ." Far from being a demand to feel lousy about our screw-ups, *metanoia* invites us to radically transform the way we perceive ourselves, others and the world... and to see with divine eyes.

So we can see now that Jesus and John the Baptist are actually calling us into an altogether different reality than that of repentance. They are calling us into a "cosmic shift in mind and heart," to higher and deeper levels of awareness and understanding.

And we can see that this shift to *metanoia* is a shift toward seeing with the eyes of a mystic, of one who can notice awe and wonder being "always nearby," of one who can see past our ego-selves and into the inclusive and all-encompassing love of God. Just as Dr. Keltner tells us, "These wonders are all around us, *if we only pause for a moment and open our mind.*"

An elusive question here now might be: But how does this happen? *How* does our mind open? How do we "open our mind" so that we might be more able to notice awe and wonder, to see more expansively and lovingly, to come to see through *metanoia* eyes?

THE PRACTICE: STILLNESS

I think the key word here from Dr. Keltner is "pause."

Because if we really want to nourish the inner mystic within us and be able to see with *metanoia* eyes, we need to consider taking our cue from people like Jesus of Nazareth and other spiritual masters—Mahatma Gandhi, Howard Thurman, Martin Luther King, Jr. and countless others, mystics among them: We must, like they do, "pause." But not just for a moment.

Spiritual masters and mystics pause, yes, but they pause... *as a consistent and intentional practice.* They pause in a simple practice of contemplative *silence and stillness*, resting in God.

I believe the call of our inner mystic invites us to do the same.

I have found the teachings of author Lerita Coleman Brown to be invaluable to me in my own practice of silence and stillness.

Dr. Brown recently wrote a book titled *What Makes You Come Alive: A Spiritual Walk with Howard Thurman.* In a recent online contemplative day that was sponsored by the *Closer Than Breath* contemplative community, she invited us into a time of silence. It was a time in which I was able to directly experience how silence can reveal moments of awe and wonder.

Dr. Brown said,

> I want to invite you to go outside for 15 minutes and see if you can *notice some stillness.*
>
> Now, stillness does not necessarily mean nothing is moving. Yes, there *is* a certain kind of sense that you pick up when things are very still. But stillness *also* can be seen in a hawk flying across the sky, or the clouds moving across the sky, or leaves falling... or you can see it in rain.
>
> If it's nighttime where you are... I'm sure you can find some stillness out there. Stars are very still.
>
> Or if you cannot go outside right now, see if you can imagine a place where you feel encompassed by stillness.
>
> Or see if you can find the stillness in yourself.
>
> And if you can feel the stillness, see if you can *bask* in it, see if you can be *embraced* by it... it's *there.*

THE PRACTICE: CENTERING PRAYER

Henri Nouwen spoke to how such a quiet, wordless, contemplative prayer practice of silence can awaken us to see with *metanoia* eyes. He says,

The practice of contemplative prayer is the discipline by which we begin to "see" the living God dwelling in our own hearts ... The divine Spirit alive in us makes our world transparent for us and *opens our eyes to the presence of the divine Spirit in all that surrounds us.*

Nouwen's words here are an invitation to nurture the inner mystic within each of us and to maintain for ourselves a *consistent and intentional* contemplative practice that gets us where the inner mystic within us longs for us to be—able to open our eyes to the presence of the divine Spirit in all that surrounds us, to *the awe and wonder that is always nearby.*

I believe that in our modern day and time, the closest we can come to a practice that can foster in us the *metanoia* way of being that was Jesus's way, and the way of the mystics before and after him, is by practicing the new but ancient practice of **Centering Prayer**, a "resting in God" meditative practice of silence and stillness.

Centering Prayer embodies the same interior, self-emptying, kenotic pause of Jesus' own contemplative practice of taking time apart to be in silence "in" God, (as Jesus actually instructed us to pray in Matthew 6:6—in our own "inner room"). And the transformative pause-release-return practice of Centering Prayer is enjoying a surge of interest today for Christians and non-Christians alike, and in both spiritual and neuroscientific circles.

Indeed, there is much that is fascinating and even thrilling about the transformative practice of Centering Prayer and its connection to scripture, psychology, and science. For a deep dive into its riches, there are many excellent books and many online sources available—I particularly recommend the *Closer Than Breath* online community and Contemplative Outreach as a beginning, and also as a way to engage in a Centering Prayer practice with others.

Here is a quick thumbnail sketch to give you a sense of the very simple but profound practice itself—

Centering Prayer is a very simple but profound method of Christian meditation that leads us into the quiet "stilling" of contemplative prayer. In the usually twenty to thirty minutes of designated time for the practice, we allow ourselves to rest in a silent place beyond thinking, "a kind of oasis in a day of emotional turmoil."

When thoughts arise as they always do, we let them pass through our awareness and, ever so gently, we return to a sacred word we have chosen that reminds us to consent and open ourselves again to an awareness of God's presence and action within.

·•·•••·••··

AND AS CYNTHIA BOURGEAULT tells us,

> Every time you are willing to release a thought, to perform the gesture of self-emptying, this gesture is patterned and strengthened within you. In time, with patience and persistence, it begins to take shape as *a magnetic center* within you, a deeper pull or gravitation that is clearly perceptible, like a tug to center.

A deeper pull or gravitation that is clearly perceptible, like a tug to center.

Ah, notice! Are we not catching yet another glimpse here of "something deeply hidden," something that "underlies our reality" and keeps our inner mystic compasses always pointing north?

I invite you to "come and see."

Blessings, all.

---

1. A. T. Robertson, *Word Pictures in the New Testament—2 Corinthians* (Grand Rapids, MO: Christian Classics Ethereal Library), November 14, 2014.

7

THE INCARNATE SUBJECTIVITY OF CHRIST

Shawn Ellison

"O Consuming Fire, Spirit of Love, overshadow me, so that the Word may be as it were, incarnate again in my soul. May I be for him a new humanity in which he can renew all his mystery"

— St. Elizabeth of the Trinity

•••••••••

THE INAUGURAL REVELATION

IN MY OWN TRADITION of Christian Mysticism, the abiding or habitual awareness of the divine reality underlying personal subjectivity is known as Theosis, the Unitive State, or Mystical Union with God. As a young, emergent Christian mystic, I first glimpsed my natural oneness with God in the immediacy of baptism. Upon ascending from the baptismal waters, my personal subjectivity or individuated sense of "I" was momentarily inhibited by an enforced state of abeyance. There was no self-referential thought, emotional reactivity, or somatic constriction, rather my mind was gently absorbed, powerfully transfixed by a unitive vision that diffused extraordinary bliss throughout my body. Though the mind was enraptured beyond its native reflexivity, it was dynamically present and clear with the body cosmically and pervasively extended everywhere at once. The undeniable impression of a transcendent power, or divine grace, which countenanced this experience, existed as a palpable "background knowledge"—inducing humility, reverence, and indebtedness to the Divine.

While this mystical reality was undoubtedly timeless, infinitely spacious, and ecstatic, when I returned to my usual orientation of individuated self-awareness and physical locality, I realized the experience only lasted under a minute. Returning to myself felt like the peaceful descent of a feather upon the contracted density of personal subjectivity. As I exited the baptism pool, I was interiorly discombobulated, for with the return of the empirical self and its vast personal subjectivity, I was flooded with overwhelming thoughts, questions, feelings, and emotions. I was principally concerned with two inquiries: 1) "What is the nature of this divine reality?" And 2) "What is the identity of that which knows and is one with this reality?" In the experience, I was truly undifferentiated, having no sense of personal identity or interior subjectivity. The identity of the enigmatic knower, its mysterious knowing, and the incandescent reality of oneness known were inexplicable.

As a deeply religious 15-year-old Protestant, I had never heard of mysticism, contemplation, or higher states of consciousness. Hence, I did not have the experiential vocabulary to frame and articulate my experience for several years later. After this inaugural revelation of mystical oneness, I possessed the incontrovertible certitude that there was more to God or Absolute Truth than I was conditioned to believe and embarked with the full force of my being to persistently actualize what was revealed. Still, I desperately longed to know the numinous subjectivity that absorbed my own into its impenetrable silence and mystery. I was keenly aware that intellectual, philosophical, or theological extrapolations of this unknown subjectivity would have been woefully inadequate. It was obvious that its ultimate revelation and experiential stabilization was contingent upon a sublime order of grace that transcended the limitations of the mind, its intractable striving, and the entanglements of personal subjectivity.

MYSTICAL UNION WITH GOD
THE UNITIVE STATE

The six years following my baptism were phenomenally marked by a mystical intensity that stretched my human limits of endurance. Visions, locutions, raptures, ecstasies, divine absorptions, variations of contemplative presence, wounds of love, invisible stigmata, the hound of heaven, direct communion with departed saints, sensational energies that ravaged the body, automatic writing, glossolalia, Eucharistic revelations, and much more became unusually commonplace. At the height of this mystical intensity during my senior year of college, an invisible, membranous film descended upon my mind, shrouding its faculties of knowing in darkness. The mystical descent of the cloud of unknowing initiated a silent implosion of my interior life with God, which formed a black hole, void, or emptiness in the center of my personal subjectivity. Every mystical experience abruptly disappeared and I found myself ontologically impaired. Far more traumatic was the vanishing of the inner sense of God's presence underlying all experience—a deeply felt awareness of God's immanent presence in myself.

By this transitional landmark in Christian contemplative process—St. John of the Cross' passive dark night of the spirit—I was thoroughly educated on the major milestones of the mystical journey. Without the privilege of a spiritual director or the insulation of the monastery, I was gracefully guided by the contemplative genius of the Christian mystical tradition itself. The brilliant works of St. Teresa of Avila, St. John of the Cross, Madame Jeanne Guyon, and Bernadette Roberts were my unfailing, essential guides. However, possessing the navigational tools to successfully move through the passive night of the spirit does not mitigate the immense psychological, emotional, and spiritual suffering encountered in the interior depths of the soul. Of the innumerable, transforming effects of the passive night of the spirit, the direct revelation of how beloved, cherished, and accepted by God we truly are in our complete humanity, is one of the greatest.

This is a metamorphic revelation that heralds the end of the passive night of the spirit. It is a revelation that occurs after the soul has encountered and integrated the bottomless void of its own nothingness. In a word, an ontological nothingness that can only be manifested in the dissolution of our egoic dimension of self-awareness and the disintegration of our subtle feeling of personal existence. In Psalm 42—an experiential accounting of this passive night of the spirit—the Psalmist cried out: "Deep calls to deep in the roar of your waterfalls; all your waves and breakers have swept over me" (v. 7). When I encountered the "rock bottom" abyss of my being—the deepest ground of my existence—God climactically revealed that the singular nothingness residing at the center of my soul is the same universal, divine nothingness out of which I was created. Thus, when "deep calls to deep in the roar of God's waterfalls," we learn by unmediated revelation that this interior convergence of nothingness is the indistinct union of our created form with the uncreated form of the Divine.

Although it would take several volumes to articulate the profundity of the passive night of the spirit and its pivotal transitions, this night comes to an enchanting conclusion in Stanza XXII of St. John of the Cross' exemplary Spiritual Canticle:

> The bride has entered
> The pleasant and desirable garden,
> And there reposes to her heart's content;
> Her neck reclining
> On the sweet arms of the Beloved (p. 94).

This explicit juncture in the Spiritual Canticle is the commencement of Full Union with God or The Unitive Revelation. Before the unitive revelation, we have directly encountered by grace the divine nothingness at the center of our being and our intrinsic oneness with that divine nothingness. Notwithstanding, the revelation of this transformative convergence does not terminate the passive night of the spirit, rather it provides the domestic basis for a more radical integration of consciousness. Deep within the recesses of being, I saw, I knew, that my union with God utterly transcended all former variations of "mystical experience." In Truth, the simple reality of union with God is a luminous and abiding seeing into the immanent depths of our own existence indistinguishable from God's existence.

However, to secure this luminous seeing without the requisite of deliberate effort or mindful concentration, the exterior faculties of the soul (memory, emotion, imagination, and intellect) must be subordinated to the redemptive energies of union itself. The faculty of will had already passed into divine union at the interior convergence of nothingness, which is the epistemological backbone of the luminous seeing of the unitive state. This mystical seeing is akin to a perpetual contemplation of an unclouded, nebulous light in the center of ourselves. In the passive night of the spirit, the exterior faculties wander incessantly, unable to surrender to the formless, divine nothingness in the depths of being. One day, unknowingly advanced in this redemptive phase of unification, I sensed the unexpected, ethereal movement of a delectable breeze, reminiscent of God "walking in the garden in the cool of the day" (Genesis 3:8). Astounded, I paused what I was doing and placed my complete attention on this indescribable breeze that serenely and delightfully swept across the innermost parts of my being.

Many revelations occurred in this unforgettable moment, but preeminent among them all, was the buoyant, vigorous uplifting of my soul high above itself and into the boundless depths of God. This was not a rapture, ecstasy, or out-of-body experience, but the elevation of my humanity into its immaculate, original configuration and the subsequent descent of my transformed humanity into the concreteness of bodily form. After this transformed, original humanity was integrated and established in my embodiment, there was an exquisite reverberation that fluidly echoed a glorious radiance of divinization throughout my being. In essence, this reverberation was the divine effect of "The Kiss of His Mouth" (Song of Solomon 1:2), which is the contemplative diffusion of the unitive strength, chastity, power, virtue, possession, and authority. St. John of the Cross describes this marital event as a "Confirmation in grace"—the irrevocability of unitive awareness—whereby the soul can never lose her abiding consciousness of God in the center of her being.

THE UNITIVE DILEMMA

Upon the onset of the abiding unitive state, I initially believed some unknown aspect of my own personal subjectivity participated in union with God. After all, the experience of the passive dark night of the spirit that disclosed my supernatural union with God was entirely mine. The sudden falling away of my egoic dimension of existence, the tremendous psychological and emotional suffering, the unfathomable confrontation with my own nothingness, the direct encounter with mysterious ontological forces that create the very reality of sin and separateness, the immense, physical strain placed upon my faculties of knowing, and many challenges unnamed, were evidently derived from personal experience. Hence, my union with God, in which the Divine was experientially revealed as closer to me than my own flesh and blood, felt radically personal. It was clear that the experience of union with God—the overflowing, uninterrupted divine awareness, the raging, living flame of love rising unceasingly from my innermost parts, the peace that surpasses understanding as a fixed property of being, and joy unspeakable imbued with every breath—was also mine.

However, inspired by the groundbreaking work of the late Christian contemplative Bernadette Roberts (1931-2017), I recognized that there was a hidden form of self-gratification in the experience of divine union itself. Cut from the same contemplative cloth as Bernadette, I'd learned to give All to God and retain nothing as a fundamental criterion of unconditional love for God. In other words, to serve and love God without mystical experiences is the sincerest and highest goal of the Christian spiritual life. In becoming increasingly aware of this subtle self-gratification present in the unitive state, I began to practice conscious detachment from the phenomenal experiences endemic to the unitive state.

This practice of detachment not only included the primary experiences of divine union aforementioned, but the underlying gift of the unitive state, which allowed me to volitionally enter the beatific vision of the Godhead whenever time permitted. In Christian mystical theology, the beatific vision is the unveiled glory of the Trinity prior to, behind, and beyond the universe. This ecstatic experience is unimaginable and immeasurably transcendent. It cannot be procured by any artificial means, spiritual technologies, postures of prayer, or meditative practices. The volitional accessibility to the beatific vision is pure, unmediated grace; a divine, consolatory gift of the unitive state to participate in our eternal destiny in the Godhead whenever we desire.

Nonetheless, I realized that spending my whole unitive life volitionally and, sometimes, involuntarily, in superlative ecstasy was insidiously hedonistic. The subtle gratification derived from the beatific vision was a narcissistic secret embedded in the unitive state; a self-indulgent clinging onto a piece of heaven that encouraged disinvolvement from the ordinary, mundane dimension of earthly life. Consequently, to pass into a deeper reality of the unitive state and, by extension, a more selfless Union with God, I felt mysteriously compelled to relinquish the ecstatic glories of heaven. The only obstacle to this daring relinquishment was that since the mystical portal to heaven was isolated deep in the interior of union, the permanent closure of this portal was strictly a divine prerogative. As I had grown accustomed in the contemplative life, I had to patiently wait for God to act within me.

THE INCARNATE SUBJECTIVITY OF CHRIST

The mystical portal had an irresistible, magnetic pull on my conscious center of attention, often resulting in an annihilative blackout as heaven powerfully overcame my terrestrial existence. Notwithstanding, I

could at least practice detachment. Some months after I made the au-
dacious decision to relinquish the mystical portal to God's own beatific
dimension of existence, I knelt in prayer. As always, I held the desire to
relinquish the portal at the forefront of my hopeful heart with open,
surrendered intention. There I faithfully waited, hoping for God to
extract this wonderful gift from the unitive state that had unexpectedly, for many undisclosed reasons, become an insurmountable obstacle
to functional earthly living. After a few minutes of gazing within at
the nebulous, divine light in the center of being—an advanced form of
unitive prayer—I felt an interior disturbance on the level of the divine
ground Itself that resembled a volcanic rumbling. Without warning,
the interior vision of the nebulous, divine light—habitually so resplen-
dent, immense, and wide—began retracting quickly, collapsing into
itself as its brightness proportionately dimmed.

Immediately, I feared that I was losing the unitive state because the
inconceivable retraction of divine light felt like the tragic onset of
another spiritual death from which, I thought I would never recover.
The holistic devastation of the passive night of the spirit was relatively
fresh in my mind. Given the historical nature of my proclivity toward
intense, ontological fluctuation that, by the grace of God, I've repeat-
edly survived, my concerns were not without justification. Holding
my breath in absolute suspense, my interior gaze immovably fixed on
this bewildering retraction of divine light, I saw the light reduced to a
diminutive speck of luminosity. Around this speck of luminosity was
total darkness and unknowing—analogous to beholding empty space
with a singular star shining faintly from an unquantifiable distance.

Once the retraction of divine light, namely, God within, ceased, there
was an impregnated silence in the anticipation of what might happen
next. I felt a tight knot in my abdomen as my interior gaze focused on

the luminous speck of divine light—my gaze sometimes peripherally drifting to appraise the pervasive space that surrounded the light. Even with the intermittent drifting of my interior gaze, the luminous speck of light commanded the majority of my attention. Then abruptly, the speck of light vehemently exploded outwards, fully replete with a distinct human form—a divinely possessed human nature—that was entirely differentiated from my own. As this human form exponentially dispersed itself from the deepest ground of my existence, mystically possessing every molecule of my embodied existence, I was wordlessly overcome by the inconceivable simplicity, grandeur, and exquisiteness of such a sublime, majestic form.

Instinctively, I knew without qualm or the slightest hesitation that this glorified human form was not "me," my personal subjectivity, nor the divine ground of consciousness, rather it was a revelatory identity that could not be mistaken or misappropriated as anything else. When the mystical possession of this glorified human form was complete, my personal subjectivity was forcibly displaced. The delusion of appropriating any aspect of divine union with God to my personal subjectivity was dismantled and hurled to oblivion. What was revealed in the immutable void and displacement of personal subjectivity was the Incarnate Christ—God's human form. It was revealed that the Incarnate Christ is the divine subjectivity that is eternally one with the Triune Godhead: the Unmanifest Transcendent, the Manifest Logos, and the Manifesting Spirit. Unbeknownst to personal subjectivity, the Incarnate Christ alone was the mystical reality in me that was definitively one with God in the unitive state.

Thus, the Incarnate Christ is the mysterious, divine junction in which the nothingness of human nature and the nothingness of divine nature eternally converge in oneness. Indeed, this mystical revelation was "the mystery which has been hidden from ages and from generations, but now has been revealed...Christ in you, the hope of glory" (Colossians 1:26-27). When I opened my eyes, I looked bafflingly at my hands, stunned into silent submission as the recapitulated birth of the Incarnate Christ in my soul gloriously infiltrated my whole embodiment. In a surreal flash of instantaneous recognition, it was strangely evident: It was no longer "I" that lived, but Christ that lives in me (Galatians 2:20). As elegantly expressed by St. Elizabeth of the Trinity, I became a "new humanity" for Christ to "renew all of His incarnate mystery." The essential mystery of this new humanity is the Truth of Christ—the incarnate oneness of divine and human natures in Christ. It was the Incarnate Christ as God's human form that I unknowingly encountered in the aftermath of my baptism—a divine truth that could not adhere without sufficient preparation. Baptism, then, is our graced participation in the Incarnate Mystery of Christ as a fait accompli and the initiation of a mystical process by which our transformation into the divine subjectivity of the Incarnate Christ becomes an abiding reality in the here and now.

Paradoxically, the Revelation of the Incarnate Christ in the unitive state is the pinnacle of human dissatisfaction because it effectively dissolves all self-appropriation—however divine or exalted we believed the Self to be. There is no "me," "I," or "myself" to be one with God, rather Christ alone is our eternal oneness with God. There's a crucifying sense of having been excommunicated from the divine union—my personal subjectivity relegated to a passive witness of a union that transcends me in every way. This particular revelation of Christ in the Christian mystical tradition is also referred to as the Consummation of the Spiritual Marriage. Madame Jeanne Guyon profoundly explicates in her wonderful commentary on the Song of Solomon:

> But as regards the communication of
> the Word to the soul,
> I say that the soul must first have arrived in God alone,
> and been there established in essential union,
> and by the spiritual marriage,
> before the divine communication
> can be made to it; as the fruits and products of marriage
> can only appear after its consummation (p. 19).

It is this lofty and transcendent communication of the Incarnate Word to the soul that ushers in Bernadette Roberts' Critical Turning Point of the unitive life, whereby the Incarnate Christ becomes our dominant subjectivity in Its ultimate return to the Godhead. As the divine powerlessness of the soul increases in the unitive state, God's human form assumes and transubstantiates our original human form: "Christ must increase, but I must decrease" (John 3:30). My immediate question following this shattering revelation was: "How could my personal subjectivity contend with the unbelievable reality of the Incarnate Christ?" In this union of substitution, I realized that my personal subjectivity and the relative, empirical self from which it arose, were inevitable sacrifices on the altar of Christ's total preeminence over all things.

Again, I resonated mystically with St. Paul when he exclaimed: "I regard everything as loss because of the surpassing value of knowing Christ. For his sake I have suffered the loss of all things, and I regard them as rubbish, in order that I may gain Christ..." (Philippians 3:8).

Therefore, to be a contemplative follower of Christ, the divine subjectivity of God's human form must be mystically revealed by the transforming power of the Holy Spirit. We must come to know that the Incarnate Christ alone is the inner knowing of the Godhead's immanent life. In the unsearchable, interior depths of our essential union with God, the Mystery of Christ is incarnated by the grace of baptism as our inner path to Trinitarian beatitude. In its recapitulated unfolding through our own human adventure, the incarnate subjectivity of Christ gradually transforms our humanity into Its own glorified humanity in the Trinity.

8

BECOMING THE EVERYDAY MYSTIC
Jen and Phil Wood

THE PLAN WAS TO resign from the church, sell the house, move, and figure it out one step at a time.

We sat with this plan for six weeks thinking, discerning and praying. We got COVID at that time. It was the first round in December of 2020 and it slowly moved one person at a time through our entire family. That season was so hard and scary. One of my sons ended up in an Emergency Room because he couldn't breathe. Another lost his taste and smell for a year. We ended up not leaving our house for a month. It really took us down, but it also created so much space to think and talk.

We processed this massive life decision every day. Forty days seemed appropriate. After all, there were forty days in the wilderness, forty years in the desert and forty days of Lent every year as a season of deep processing. In the end, something within told us it was time to go- we just knew it.

We sat our three boys down first and told them that we were leaving. There were tears and confusion which was to be expected. It was all they had ever known as well.

"Why?!"

"We have other work we need to do."

"You are crazy! You guys built this. You spent so long building this. How could you leave it?"

"Because we have grown and it is time to go. We have to keep going."

"What are you going to do to make money?"

"We have some ideas. We created this from nothing; we will create whatever is next. We are going to try a bunch of stuff."

"Hope it makes money. Have you told anyone?"

"No."

After that, we told the leadership team at the church, set up transition, there was a final Sunday and then we left.

And just like that, a twenty-year season and way of life ended.

After we left the church, we had been leading for the past dozen years, not only did our souls ache, but we were left feeling disoriented and even confused. There are clear steps for starting and leading a church, but out in the wild, with no clear next steps before us, while it felt exhilarating and free, it also was terrifying. Even though we knew it was time to leap and the right thing for us to do—it was no less scary.

How would we continue to serve people, continue to help them grow in a fresh way and also pay the bills?

How would we continue to use our gifting and all we had learned leading the last 20 years and also create something new that felt authentic to the people we were expanding into?

While we had lots of ideas, we were unclear exactly what to do next. And what we realized is that our old fallback of polling others, putting people into places of authority in our lives then asking them what to do, and asking for permission would no longer work for us in this new space.

It was time to trust ourselves and the Spirit that had always been guiding us- to really trust our intuition in a new way- the way mystics had done for thousands of years. The essence of mysticism boils down to cultivating a life that allows for a heightened awareness and direct experience of the divine within ourselves and in the world around us.

Most of our own adult lives, we had both been looking everywhere else for direction, validation and wisdom, and what we came to realize was that the answer was right in front of us all along. In our lives, for too long, we gave away our own agency in determining influence in our life. And it let us down again and again. We voluntarily put people over our own lives and gave them influence and authority over us in unhealthy ways. We'd look to them for answers, permission and approval, even when deep down we already knew what we needed to do. It caused us great anxiety and it kept us from actually stepping into the full life, wisdom, divinity and Spirit authority that we already had.

It was actually already inside of us. And the answer is inside of you too.

We each have our own authority right here and now.

We experienced a profound shift of recognizing the Spirit within and recognizing our own inner authority versus trying to please and gain permission from any kind of external authority in our life. This changed everything for us. It is one thing to talk about it, know this in your head, even preach about it- and it is another thing altogether to live from that kind of inner awareness, wisdom and authority in the real world. As we began to lean into our inner wisdom, we found that each step was revealed to us- one step at a time.

When you are building a new life, which we were from the ground up, you have to learn to become acutely aware of your internal world. If you don't, you can accidentally find yourself looking for permission or approval for your new life from others or worse yet- living out old unhealthy cycles repeating the past again and again.

In psychological terms, this is called Interoception.

It is our eighth sense and it allows us to feel or sense the inside of our bodies. This is inner body awareness. Interoception is a relatively new concept with extensive research but low general population awareness. We have receptors in our internal organs and tissues that gather information from those organs in order to send it to our brain for processing.

Our inner body awareness helps us with things like knowing when we need to use the bathroom, what tickles or itches, body pains, muscle tightness, heart rate fluctuations, etc. But, because our emotions are experiences that happen in our bodies, interoception is how you feel your emotions.

Every emotion brings different feelings and sensations in different parts of your body. Through inner body awareness, you learn to identify, name, feel, and move emotions through and out of your body. It helps you identify what is happening beneath the surface and it impacts everything from decision making to conversation, social awareness, intuition, perspective, empathy, self awareness and self-regulation.

We have an entire world of emotion happening in our bodies and without the ability to access that world, regulate it, and operate with it, you can find yourself stuck or dysregulated, or even disempowered again and again. This how we end up trapped in prisons of our own making through unprocessed and unregulated thoughts, self-talk, and emotions. They can get triggered or even stuck in our bodies and cause us a world of dysfunction and harm.

This is how you end up in fights with your partner or kids or coworkers or family or friends in extremes that are out of proportion to the argument, or trapped in unforgiveness and bitterness. This is how anxiety gets stuck in your body and can't get out as you live in a perpetual state of fight or flight. It is more than a thought; it is a whole body experience.

Often, we can find ourselves overly sensitive or overly numb to our inner world. In order to learn how to access and work with your inner world, you have to build self-awareness. You can do this by sitting in silence and paying attention to what you feel inside, where you feel it and what it is saying to you.

You can identify those thoughts, feelings and emotions and name them. For emotions or anxiety that feel stuck, you can move your body through walking or exercise to flush them physically out of it. You can also find a good therapist or coach that does embodiment work to help you learn these skills and hone them.

This is one of the reasons why we got into breathwork and thermal exposure—to learn to connect with, identify, work with and regulate our internal states. When you practice different forms of breathwork and get into a freezing ice bath it very quickly connects your head with your body.

It is not just woo-woo (although it is in all the best ways) and it's not just an instagrammable moment (although it's definitely that as well). There is research that shows that we have two brains, or neurological centers, in our body. One in our head and one in our gut. Inner body awareness literally connects our heads and our thoughts with our bodies and emotions and sets us free. It is a learned integration. You can learn to pay attention to your body- it is always talking to you.

During breathwork, you often see pent up emotions come out involuntarily through crying, laughing or physical sensation both in yourself and in others. Stuff just comes out. Culturally, we live in our heads and when you learn embodiment practices to develop your interoception, it connects you back to your body while setting you free in the process.

The difficulty of your experience in an ice bath, hot sauna or on a mat doing breathwork depends largely on the level of anxiety and emotion that you are carrying. I have seen people jump out of the ice bath onto the ground or writhe in pain while others sit calmly like a monk in meditation. When you learn to control your breath and subsequently your emotions in an ice-bath, you can learn to regulate and control them anywhere.

One friend that works in finance said he got so good at identifying and controlling his inner world through these experiences that his managers at his stressful work environment noticed the difference and asked how he was operating the way that he was in such stressful situations.

People notice when you set yourself free.

There is nothing more depleting than living with trapped emotions and the inability to access and regulate your internal world. But on the other hand, it is wildly empowering to connect your head and your heart, access your inner world, set yourself free, and hyper charge your connection with others as well as your own life.

It isn't just psychological; it is also spiritual.

You can learn to access your inner wisdom within. Everything is spiritual and while the psychological and spiritual are both deeply interconnected and difficult to pull apart, we do make a distinction and believe it is important to make. Developing a strong sense of Interoception gives you the tools you need to access the Spirit within.

Jesus is recorded as saying a very mystical and profound thing: "I am in my Father, and you are in me, and I am in you." (John 14:20)

He is pretty clear in how he sees things. He and God are one; he only does what God is doing. He speaks and acts on the authority of God, not even his own. And then he goes as far as to say—I am in my Father, and you are in me, and I am in you.

Whatever God is, all of that is in us.

That same God-ness and divine life, even to the degree that he says you will do what God does and even greater things, is in us.

Think about that. Let that settle in.

That divine spark and animating Spirit is within you.

The Tradition we come from calls this Christ in you. It also says you are hidden in Christ.

Consider the other places Jesus speaks about this. "...he breathed on them and said, 'Receive the Holy Spirit. If you forgive anyone's sins, their sins are forgiven; if you do not forgive them, they are not forgiven.'" (John 20:21-13)

Spirit is within you; you have the power to breathe life, create love and forgive sins, or not.

In another place he says don't worry what you will say, Spirit will tell you. He speaks of Spirit giving immense power, discernment and the heaven binding power of interpretation, which is simply discerning what Spirit is actually doing in you and in the world in your own day and age and then acting on it. That is a lot of trust; that's a lot of inner wisdom.

This is a very clear description and expectation by Jesus.

He gives us his Spirit and trusts us with that Spirit.

And with that comes divine power, wisdom and life.

You have the Spirit in you. You can trust your own inner wisdom.

Many of us have been taught, conditioned and trained that we are bad and that we can't trust ourselves. But Jesus is pretty clear on this.

You are good and trustworthy.

You are holy and divine.

You possess a profound inner wisdom.

We are a part of a culture and a 1600 year old religious tradition of conditioning in which we have been taught to look to religious and spiritual leaders to tell us who God is, what to do, how to read sacred texts, and how to live our lives and be "good." They have served as a sort of divine power or authority over our lives and on some level it's robbed humanity of its God given inner wisdom and power. We often give our own power over to others and forget that we each have the ability to tap into a deep well of inner wisdom and God-given authority.

But, the movement didn't begin this way. Jesus clearly didn't give this impression.

Roughly 400 years after Jesus, an influential leader in the Church movement named Augustine introduced a novel concept called Original Sin. In spite of Jesus' original invitation, he offered the idea that humanity is inherently bad. This idea stuck and ever since it has deeply impacted the Western mind.

For 1600 years we have been conditioned to believe that we can't trust ourselves or our inner wisdom or the Spirit within. When you believe that you are born a sinner, inherently bad and damned to hell and you can't trust yourself, then you need others to tell you how to think and what to do.

We've had this conversation with a lot of people learning to take back their authority and trust their inner wisdom. Jesus went to great lengths to let you know that he gave you his Spirit and that you can trust yourself and your own inner knowing.

By owning your inner wisdom, you are not rejecting Jesus or his path, you are owning the actual Jesus vision. You are embodying it. You are taking it more seriously.

Jesus gave us immense power and authority and somewhere along the way, many of us gave it up. But, there is a shift happening- people are waking up to what has always been true. You have the Spirit within. You can access and trust your God-given inner wisdom.

You don't need to look to others to approve of you or your life or to tell you what to do. Only you can do that for yourself.

You have what you need. You can trust yourself.

You are not rejecting community or tradition or other people by owning your wisdom. You are stepping fully into your part of it. People fully empowered is what church actually is. It's putting the power back in the hands of the people.

Often, without practice, we can find ourselves unfamiliar with or unaware of our inner wisdom. In order to learn how to access and work with it, just like interoception, it takes practice. You have to build a different kind of self-awareness through silence, meditation, embodiment practices, contemplation and by paying attention to what you sense inside and what it is saying to you.

You can journal those thoughts, feelings and sensations and name them.

Try it—take time for yourself to sit in silence and quiet your mind. Be still. Breathe. And listen to your inner knowing. Give space to become aware.

Listen for what comes up. Pay attention to your body- get in touch with your senses. Our bodies are often the first place where we feel our intuition. It can be in the stomach, or in the tightening of your chest, or an opening and release of tension. Think about what happens to your body when you're with your safest person. What happens to your body? Can you feel it relax and uncoil? Do you feel open or a release?

Now think about being with an unsafe person in your life. What happens in your body? Is it tense? Are your teeth clenched? Are you bracing? Your body can provide valuable information through physical sensations like gut feelings, tension, or relaxation. Pay attention to these cues and consider what they might be indicating. Embodiment practices help with that. Being present in our bodies and paying attention to what they are saying can help us understand what's going on in us and what we need to do next. What's your body saying to you and where is it saying it?

Pay attention to your emotions. You can journal and write out your thoughts, feelings, and experiences which can help you process your emotions and uncover your inner knowing. Regular journaling can assist in making connections and revealing patterns in your thinking.

Emotions can act as signals that provide insight into your inner knowing. Notice any emotional reactions to situations and reflect on what they might be telling you. Emotions can be a great indicator of what we are feeling. When emotions rise up within you, what might they be saying? If you get super mad about something, for instance, ask what's going on there? You don't need to allow your emotions to rule you, but you can listen to what they might be saying to you. And then the next level of that awareness is learning how to regulate your emotions in a way that serves you.

Then practice following your gut instinct. Trust it. The more you act on your inner wisdom, the stronger it will become. Remembering past experience can help as you practice living this way. Analyze situations in which you relied on your intuition and evaluate the outcomes. This can help you trust yourself. Accessing your inner wisdom takes time and practice so be patient with yourself and recognize that it may take some time to fully tap into.

Finally, ask yourself good questions like what is the best next step before me? What is the real challenge here? What is really going on inside me?

What is your inner knowing, Spirit within, telling you? What is it telling you about your relationships or parenting or work or next steps? What is it telling you about areas you need to grow in, or who you need to become to take those steps before you? You can trust it. You already have everything you need.

Try leaning into that knowing and see what happens. We dare you.

When you quiet your mind, develop inner body awareness and learn to access and pay attention to your inner wisdom, you begin to live from what we call, your inner authority.

With inner authority you break the cycles that have had power over your life. You are free to build a life that is true to yourself because you have learned that deep down, you can trust yourself. You are free to live connected to the movements of your own soul and the Spirit within and around you.

Which turns out to be an incredibly powerful everyday mystical experience.

9
YOUR INVITATION TO THE DANCE
Tim Burnette

CONTEMPLATION IS SO MUCH more than silence, stillness, and solitude.

The inner postures that are learned in these contemplative moments are meant to be brought into the whole of life.

Contemplatives are people who learn to lean in to all that life throws their way with a spirit of welcome—that we might learn to dance with life wherever it may be charting a new path.

A number of years ago now, I remember attending a conference in Chicago called Mystic Soul, that was a contemplative gathering led by and purposed for BIPOC folks—but that also welcomed Anglo folks who were on their own decolonizing journeys as well.

My standout takeaway from the conference was from a compelling speaker named Therese Taylor-Stinson during one of the opening sessions. Her big point for the morning was that:

"Intentional acts of contemplation do not have to be silent. They can be danced, sung, or shouted. Any act that brings us to attention in Spirit is an act of contemplation."

As someone who had inquired of mystical traditions in the West—especially Western Christianity—I had encountered many invitations to be silent and still alone in solitude. That was certainly the way I was initially taught contemplative practices while in seminary.

Whether or not you also grew up in Western Christianity, there is often a pervasive impulse across many Western spiritualities that contemplation is about quiet, still, attention. We see this especially in various meditation traditions that have taken root in our time and place.

And, while there's something to be said for silence and the wisdom that is birthed from that inner place of quiet—namely, that cultivating an inner awareness can help us to see both ourselves and the events of our lives through a compassionate, nonjudgmental lens—Therese was pushing my definitions of contemplation, and unveiling how contemplation is so much more than that.

Dancing. Shouting. Anything that brings us to attention in Spirit. All of it, contemplation.

I feel that now more than ever, we need broadening definitions of contemplation—ones that are reaching to render the vastness of the inner invitations available to us in a palpable way.

One of my favorite definitions of contemplative prayer comes from mystic and teacher Richard Rohr, who says that "contemplative prayer is loving conscious union with the reality right in front of us"—which is another name for loving conscious union with what is.

This means that contemplation can be a posture that is embodied anywhere and everywhere. And obviously, to Therese Taylor-Stinson's point, it is an invitation to see contemplation as including the noisiness and movements of our everyday lives.

The goal is to tend to Spirit in whatever situation we might find ourselves. And Spirit, says

theologian Grace Ji Sun Kim, should be reimagined more

> as breath,
> as wind,
> as vibration,
>
> and as social movement.

She writes in her book, Reimagining Spirit, that:

> The world is filled with Spirit. One can feel its presence
> everywhere. The Spirit is not owned by anyone, and we
> certainly cannot say that it is the sole possession of Chris-
> tians. For, the Spirit is free and moves where it will.

If you'll notice with me for a moment, all the images that she uplifts for
Spirit are about movement—which are poetic images that are trying to
express something like aliveness. And, since there is no such thing as a
disembodied spirituality—we are thus invited to tune in to this sense
of freshness and aliveness in our everyday lives.

From this perspective of bringing a loving, conscious, union with
"what is" to everything we go through—walking, painting, cleaning,
running, playing, singing, caregiving—anything can be an act of contemplation.

One of my favorite images of the contemplative endeavor is that of "the dance." Some people prefer "the journey," but I just love this idea of seeing spirituality as a sort of dancing. It feels more true to our changing lives.

The one statement we can make about reality is that it moves. Movement is the very heartbeat of the universe.

This we know for sure—that life is an unfolding process. Another way to say that is that life is an adventure—literally from the latin "ad/venir," meaning "to come."

To take the invitation to go on the contemplative adventure is to be oriented toward and focused on that which is to come—toward a kind of transcendence that is imminent in every moment.

In a Western culture that is so focused on being, perhaps becoming might be a better way to express what is at the heart of things.

One of my favorite philosophers made a point that, essentially, what we refer to as our "being" is really made up of "becoming," anyways.

So, why is this notion of becoming so vital to recognize? Why focus on the dance rather than the stillness?

We have been handed a domineering narrative of linearity in our time, where spirituality often gets depicted as a journey from point A to point B—something like from non-enlightenment to enlightenment. Who wouldn't like to have easily understandable map that help us find our way?

But, while this journeying from point A to point B is a modern form of clarity that helps us feel like we have a grasp on things, we have to ask ourselves the honest question of, "does that actually reflect our actual experience of our lives?"

Or, do we actually move in more circular ways?

Do we find ourselves caught up in revolutions and spirals—both up, down, and often circling back around to parts of ourselves we thought we had left behind?

Aren't we always encountering new ways to welcome ourselves?

I don't want this to be read as creating a new dualism between stillness and movement, but rather, to bring them together so we might see the truth in what the poet T.S. Eliot said, which is the wisdom of a nonduality:

> "At the still point of the turning world.
> Neither flesh nor fleshless;
> Neither from nor towards;
> at the still point, there the dance is...
> and there is only the dance."

At the still point—at that point that we aim toward in contemplative postures—we stumble upon a center that flows. What we encounter is none other than our very life—a life that is can be named as a Divine flow.

I love that author Octavia Butler says that "God is change"—because a statement like that breaks open our Western attempts to put God in a box of our own understanding.

Not only do I think that she means that God is always beyond our attempts to create an accurate snapshot of what God is like, but I think she also means that God actually is *change*.

She observed that everything that happens in our everyday life-process is held in a divine flow of Loving presence. And, if something like this is ultimately real, then dancing is the only way to be in tune with these movements.

I remember one evening in December, 2017, I was at a local brewery in Santa Barbara, CA for a curated dinner they host each year during the feast of St. Barbara. We were caught up in the flow of some beautiful courses of food and beer pairings when something jarring happened—the lights in the brewery went out.

Everyone gasped for a moment from the startling change in brightness, then started to chatter a bit, and then the staff came by and lit some candles while we slowly ended up finishing the rest of the meal in the dark by candlelight.

We didn't know why the power had gone out, but just kept going on with the meal, and had a wonderful evening.

On the way home, I was feeling the spirit of that night and was jamming to some tunes in my car when I had this sensation like, you know what? I wanna dance.

So I found this large field, and, as it was late in the evening and there was really no one around, I grabbed my phone and ear buds, and just proceeded to have a little silent disco dance party by myself on this field.

It only lasted for a couple of songs, and then I jovially got back in my car and went home. I cannot tell you why I did this, as it's not something

I've ever really done again. But I just knew that, in that moment, I had to dance with that night.

When I got home and turned on the TV, I found out that what caused the power outage was the beginning of what became the Thomas Fire here in Santa Barbara—which at the time, grew to be the largest series of wildfires in California history.

These fires turned out to be quite a catastrophic ordeal for our area, as many people lost their homes, and the fires ended up starting a chain reaction that led to the Montecito mudslides, which devastated our local community.

But, I didn't know that when I went to dance.

All I knew was that, that night, I had to dance—to dance with what I had experienced that evening, completely oblivious to the future ramifications of the blossoming wildfires that evening.

Do you have something in your life that you can't explain—even to yourself—but that you have to just do?

Maybe it was a one-time experience like this, or maybe it's something that you keep more of an intentional rhythm of doing?

Have you encountered something that you just have to do, otherwise you wouldn't be being true to yourself unless you did it?

Part of the invitation to see contemplation as an all-of-life posture is to find places where you too, can dance. Maybe not always literally—but definitely actually.

For me, in recent years "dancing" has looked like playing basketball again—which was a sport I played in college, but had given up for a while after some back injuries years ago.

Basketball has become so much more for me than just a sport—it has been a way to reunite with a language that my body spoke that had gone unused for a number of years.

It was fascinating how, when I got back out there on the court at the local YMCA, my body just sort of snapped back into its old habits—without thinking.

It has become a source of so much joy for me to meet up a couple times a week with this community of guys who have become a new lifeline for me, and to just play—to get lost in the flow of my own becoming as an attunement to Spirit.

Basketball, like anything, can be a contemplative act. It too is a space where I can bring loving conscious union and move with a bodily knowing that can only be exercised on the court.

In part, basketball is contemplation precisely because it is not so much thinking, but just playing—it is a dance of sorts.

Hardcore basketball players have this phrase where they say, "ball is life."

What "is life" for you?

What makes you come alive?

Where is there a sense of freshness, beauty, and aliveness when you look inwardly?

Maybe you write,
maybe you paint,
maybe you caregive,
maybe you bake or cook,
maybe you cycle,
maybe you run,
maybe you sing or play music,
maybe you decorate,
maybe you clean, tidy, or organize—

But whatever it is that you do—if you do it in loving presence, it is a contemplative act—and a glorious example of everyday contemplation.

In short, it is an example of the dance.

So, the big vision here is that contemplation can be anything—and everything is a part of the dance of life. The great adventure of our lives is to learn how to dance with gusto—in whatever way you uniquely dance.

Mystic teacher Thomas Merton once said:

For the world and time are the dance of God in emptiness. The silence of the spheres is the music of a wedding feast...no despair of ours can alter the reality of things; or stain the joy of the cosmic dance which is always there. Indeed, we are in the midst of it, and it is in the midst of us, for it beats in our very blood, whether we want it to or not... the fact remains that we are invited to forget ourselves on purpose, cast our awful solemnity to the winds and join in the general dance.

Merton's vision of reality is what he referred to as the "cosmic dance." I sometimes call this "mystical cosmology"—which is one way of viewing the world as a cycle of Divine Love.

This "cosmic dance" idea is his big conclusion at the end of what many consider to be his magnum opus on the contemplative life, *New Seeds of Contemplation*.

His greatest contemplative invitation is that we learn to overcome our self-preoccupation and "join the general dance."

Or, in other words—that we stop seeking our being so intently, and get busy becoming instead.

His observation is that our greatest joy is found when we can attune to—remember, be in loving, conscious union with—whatever reality is happening right in front of us. And his point is, that we must let go of our egoic self-preoccupation in order to do it!

If we can become lifelong students of this inner posture of letting go, then we can attune to the joy and Beauty of life, exactly because it is the most fundamental thing going on at any moment.

And so, if we want to live in harmony with the dance—we simply have to give into it.

The point that Taylor-Stinson, Eliot, Butler, and Merton are making is this—the truest depiction of our cosmos is that of a dance, and the practical question of "what shall we do in response to that reality?" is so simple it often goes overlooked—become a dance partner.

Have you ever tried to hit the pause button on your life?

Spoiler alert: there isn't one. And the reality is, you won't ever find one anywhere!

And so, we dance. Sometimes, we are called to bring loving, conscious union with loss. Sometimes, the dance is grief—or learning to metabolize more difficult emotions. Sometimes our bodies tell us that there is something we need to do to keep moving forward.

The dance is not always celebratory—sometimes we do what we need to do in order to return to Love.

Dancing can help us to release what our body needs to let go of, in order to come back to joy—to come back to a sense of liberation and aliveness.

A few years ago, as I was heading toward an operation, my body was carrying a lot of stress and anxiety because I had been through health challenges in the past.

In order to have a more peaceful experience, I knew that I had to try to exorcise this energy out before I went in for the procedure.

So, I went down to the beach for a walk, and when I got far enough away from where there were a lot of people, I started moaning and grunting. It was one of the more primal moments I've ever experienced. I hadn't planned on it, the sounds just sort of came out on their own.

But, just like dancing in the field, this too was not something I did on a regular basis—it was a natural response of my body to aggressively vocalize some of this anxious energy I was carrying in order to get it out.

And so I walked, and I shouted and made like physical motions with my arms—and to anyone who might have seen me doing this—I'm sure it was quite a scene.

But you know what? I was able to let go of all that anxious energy on that walk. And subsequently, I felt so much more peaceful going in for that procedure after shouting and releasing what I was carrying.

I say that in order to recognize that this is one example of saying "yes" to the dance of our lives.

Sometimes yes is playing.

Sometimes yes is grieving.

But all of it is an honoring of what is real in a spirit of love and welcome—and when we do that, no matter what form it takes, we are practicing contemplation.

We must remember that the dance of our lives is a deep mystery. And, if we're being honest, we are most mysterious to ourselves.

One of my favorite theologians, Catherine Keller, says this about the adventure of the self: "To know myself is to know that I cannot literally know myself. For in the act of knowing, I am only just coming to be."

We are always being ever-renewed. This is what it means to be alive. And, if we're really honest, often times, by the time we really get to know some past self—we are already something other—something new.

Life is an adventure in becoming something new. This is why it doesn't surprise me that the Christian Testament places so much attention on being "made new."

Jesus went around talking a lot about this odd Greek word—metanoia—which a lot of people who translate it as "repent," or, "change one's mind," miss much of the point.

It literally means, go beyond the mind.

As we attempt to be good rational animals, our minds love to boxify things—to render images that we can understand that help give us a sense of stability in an unstable world.

But Jesus' invitation was to include the rational mind, but to transcend it as well—so that we can be more fully alive.

And so, we must come to recognize the mysterious, cosmic dance for what it is—precisely because each of us are flowing forward into some new and beautiful unravelling—and it is the freshness and zest of life that makes it mysterious and sublime.

If we attempt to get to know the dance by thinking, we will likely not find ourselves in rhythm.

So, the only response to the basic fact about reality—that things change—is to dance—to see our lives as endeavors in loving welcome, so that we might move with the waves, ebbs, and flows that come our way with the cathartic joy and release of a dance party.

Every day, we are presented with an invitation to choose play over solemnity.

Every day, we are invited to bring loving, conscious, union to what is.

Every day, we can attune to the movements of Spirit by saying yes to the process.

Every day, we must embark on these tiny, mundane, contemplative adventures that take us ever-deeper into union with the Divine flow of our lives.

Every day, as an act of contemplation, we must dance.

10

ALREADY ONE WITH GOD: OPENING TO GOD AS THE GROUND OF BEING

Keith Kristich

"When God is no longer out there or over there, we have begun the mystical journey."

— Richard Rohr

· · ● ● ● ● ● · · ·

HUMANITY SUFFERS FROM A case of mistaken identity, in part, because we believe that we are ultimately separate from one another, separate from the earth, and separate from God.

We live disconnected from the earth, holding our cell phones more than we hold sacred soil. Not only have we lost a grounding connection to the earth, we've also lost touch with a consciousness connected to the cosmos. In this mistaken state of identity—egoic consciousness—the universe itself is experienced as *other* and being "out there."

But the universe is not (only) out there. The universe is here. It is now. You are—literally—the universe, unfolding in real-time. "You are that," as the Chandogya Upanishad says. Because you *are* the universe, you are *one* with the Happening that is Happening. The great *Happening* is what Rabbi Rami Shapiro calls God.

The universe—the Happening that is Happening—is the book in your hand, the food in your belly, and the beat of your heart. Just as the universe unfolds in real-time, so too God is an ever-present Reality, always here, always unfolding in the reality that is our lives. And just as you can not be separate from the universe, it is not possible to be separate from God's infinite Being.

You are a living cell in the body of God. Never separate, though it is easy to *think* that you are.

Much of conventional religion affirms our separation from God. Religion often says that heaven is above, hell is below, and earth is smack in the middle. In this mistaken worldview, the spiritual journey is portrayed as a journey that is "up and out," where we eventually get to heaven to find the Zeus-like God, a God that I like to call the Guy-in-the-Sky.

This "up and out" theology says that to "find God"—the Source of true peace and joy—we must go somewhere *other than where we are*.

But there is another way—the mystic way—a way that is not up and out but *down and in*. The contemplative way is an invitation to travel through the roots of our being toward what the German mystic Meister Eckhart called the "Ground of Being." The Ground is God's Being from which all that is emerges moment by moment. But the contemplative journey of going down and in is difficult. It is countercultural. Contemplative spirituality radically goes against the grain of the world's dominant narratives of how *to be* in the world. We live in a world that values what we do, produce, and look like, and in this world, we've mistaken ourselves for something *other than* our true selves.

We have mistaken what is nonessential and always changing for what is essential and fundamentally true. We believe we are the masks we wear, the personalities we portray and the activities we do. In short, we mistake our ego for our true Self. Ego is our essence or true Self with a little bit of makeup. Essence is that which can not be removed from us. We can remove the makeup—who we pretend to be—but we can not remove our naked face beneath it—essence.

In this state of mistaken identity, we are like a naked body mistaking itself for the clothes it temporarily wears, or a tree mistaking itself for its leaves that, come autumn, drop and wither away.

But mystics—those who have cultivated contemplative consciousness—know that this is not who we are. We are not the clothes that we wear but our *naked bodies*. We are not the busy thoughts in our minds but the open *awareness* in which thoughts emerge. We are not our ever-changing feelings but the open-heart *presence* in which feelings take place. We are not the temporary, passing clouds in the sky, but the eternal sky itself.

TAKING THE CONTEMPLATIVE TURN

The contemplative journey invites us to explore not our ego, but our essence: that which can not be removed from us. To enter this path, we must make an intentional *turn*, a contemplative turn, *away* from the masks we wear *towards* that which has always been true: our naked being. Just as nothing grows from the outside in, our spiritual journey must begin with looking for what's ultimately true: God's ever-present Being within us.

A great Rabbi once said: "If your leaders say to you 'Look! The Kingdom [of God] is in the sky!' then the birds will be there before you are.

If they say that the Kingdom is in the sea, then the fish will be there before you are. Rather, the Kingdom is within you and it is outside of you." These words of Jesus invite us to cultivate contemplative consciousness, to explore our inner being as the most intimate place to commune with the divine. Of course, God is outside of us, but the Happening that is Happening is also within.

But it's not always easy to find the great Happening within us because beyond mistaking ourselves for our activity, thoughts, or feelings, we also mistake ourselves for our beliefs. Beliefs are opinions mistaken for reality. Sometimes beliefs cloud reality more than they reveal it. I know the danger of mistaking who I *am* for the beliefs I *have*. Raised evangelical, I've had to unlearn and deconstruct a lot of religious indoctrination.

It's painful to witness your worldview unravel and long-held *beliefs* (read: *opinions*) uprooted. When our worldviews shatter, we must learn to rest in a faith that is deeper than belief. Beyond belief, *trust* must be the ground beneath our ever-changing beliefs. We must trust, or deeper yet, know, that despite our changing beliefs, there is a basic core of goodness to reality, stabilizing our uncertain world. Aren't we all "made in the image and likeness of God" after all in a world that is called "good?"

Taking the contemplative turn we find a Self that is beneath our masks, beyond emotions, beyond thoughts, and beyond belief. And this Self is rooted in God's Being, divine goodness.

Contemplative practice is how we open awareness to God's Being within. Meister Eckhart said, "The eye through which I see God is the same eye through which God sees me." Contemplative practice is about opening the inner eye, what the Christian tradition has long called the "eyes of the heart." Opening this eye, we realize that we will never find heaven "out there" until we can find it first within.

Before the rise of contemplative awareness, we take ourselves to be separate from God's Being. But with intentional contemplative practice we gradually "wake up" to our groundedness in Being, like a twig on a tree looking "inwards" remembers its inherent oneness with not only the tree, trunk, and roots, but the Ground itself.

God is your Ground. God is your Being. Contemplative practice is how we sink into Being.

And if God is the source of true joy, peace, and love, then in the mistaken mind of ego, the joy and peace we seek are said to be outside of ourselves—separate, at a distance. But the mystic knows that God—the Source of love—is closer to us than we could ever imagine. Contemplatives know that to be truly religious is to return to our roots—to know the immediacy of the Divine Presence that permeates us right where we are.

But how do we wake up to this reality? How do we open the eyes of the heart?

THINKING-FEELING-DOING

Being, not Doing is the first aim of the mystic and hence should be the first interest of the student of mysticism.

— Evelyn Underhill

We live most of our days on a seemingly endless cycle of think-ing-feeling-doing, thinking-feeling-doing. Mental chatter and over-ac-tive minds define our average mental states. If we're not overthink-ing then we are overly active with a never-ending to-do list growing longer by the minute. And emotions—overwhelming waves of emo-tions—waves we sometimes seem to drown in, and on good days, surf instead.

We've lost contact with the Ground of Reality, forgetting our roots, and living only in the chaos of our branches and the storms that surround us.

Constantly thinking-feeling-doing-thinking-feeling-doing, we over-look the background of experience: the simplicity of our *being*. We overlook the simplicity of our true Self. We pay attention to our thoughts but miss the awareness in which our thoughts take place. We pay attention to our feelings, but not the open empty presence beneath them. We pay attention to our activities, but not the beingness that grounds them. In a religious context, we pay attention to our beliefs in God, indeed, we worship our *beliefs* in God, without ever stopping to remember that our beliefs are only mental images.

In ordinary awareness, our busy minds get lost in thought, our heavy hearts get lost in emotion, and our busy bodies get lost in activity. Rarely do we find the spaciousness we need to experience the soul: beingness itself. We overlook the "I *am*" that *is* before "I am this" or "I am that". And this "I am," this inner beingness, is God's grounding reality in us. God shines in us, indeed *as* us, from the inside out.

We are living expressions of an incarnate universe.

To say that we "overlook the background of experience," God as the Ground of Being, is similar to how we might overlook empty space.

Right now you are overlooking the *space between* your eyes and the words you read. You don't "see" the space because its emptiness is the container in which we look. But the space between your eyes and the words is obviously there and you are always seeing it—we simply don't give it our attention.

Similarly, we don't notice the silence in our favorite songs. We overlook the pause between the beats, missing the fact that without the silence as its background, such sound would be incoherent. Just as emptiness is the background of form and silence is the background to all sound, *God is the background of all experience*, overlooked, but nonetheless there. What appears as emptiness is revealed as a hidden fullness, as any good Buddhist will tell you: an empty cup is overflowing with air! So while we are caught up attending to our thoughts, emotions and activities, God is quietly there as the very background of experience itself: the "empty" air that *fills* the cup.

To cultivate contemplative consciousness—to tune into Being—we cease overlooking the background of experience and open our awareness to that which is ever present. We open to the God that always is. Simply is. Is "is-ness" itself. God is the ever-present background of Being in which thinking, feeling, and doing take place.

It is the mystic that knows – beyond belief – that underneath the thinking-feeling-doing-self is *being*. Bare-naked-being. And Being, as the mystery author of *The Cloud of Unknowing* writes, "is God," In contemplative prayer and deep meditation, we simply open to this Being, open to God.

But if this is true, then how do we realize this for ourselves? Is this not all just a bunch of spiritual woo?

CONTEMPLATIVE PRAYER
CAPITAL-P-PRAYER

Meditation and contemplative prayer are methods of cultivating contemplative consciousness, ways of turning towards the Ground of Being. They are ways of turning away from our small self and remembering our rootedness in God. Contemplative prayer is how we realize that we are *already* one with God.

When we know we are already one with God, there is nowhere to go, nothing to do, and no-thing to believe to *become* one with God. Contemplation becomes a simple practice of *presence*: the awareness of the inner Light of God within ourselves and within all that is.

Caroline Oakes, author of *Practice the Pause*, a book exploring cutting-edge brain science on contemplative practice, writes: "The spiritual journey begins with a pause, a centering-in-God pause, and over time becomes a constant and ceaseless 'prayer,' an honoring of and a connection with the Divine in you that awakens your essential self." Where does the spiritual journey begin? With a pause. A moment. A centering. While the journey may begin with a pause, over time this pause expands, permeating life, becoming *ceaseless*—without end.

The spiritual journey ultimately becomes our everyday lives.

What starts as sporadic moments of contemplative awareness deepens into a ceaseless prayer—a prayer you can imagine that is *always going on* in the background of experience. We might call this form of prayer, capital-P-Prayer. Prayer that is alive with awareness, presence, and being.

Capital-P-Prayer is the Prayer of birds Singing, the river Flowing, the sky Storming, and the universe Birthing. Birthing you and I. Moment by moment. God's infinite Being, unfolding, becoming you and I in real-time.

Contemplative prayer is how we consciously participate in the Prayer that is always happening.

HOW TO PRAY: STOP PRAYING

Prayer is not ultimately about words. Prayer is about relationship. It's how we deepen our relationship with the divine. Anything that takes you deeper becomes prayer. In prayer, words can sometimes help and at other times, just get in the way.

Thomas Merton put it this way:

> *It is a risky thing to pray, and the danger is that our very prayers get between God and us. The great thing in prayer is not to pray, but to go directly to God. If saying your prayers is an obstacle to prayer, cut it out... The best way to pray is: stop. Let prayer pray within you, whether you know it or not.*

Do you want to Pray?

Stop.

Stop the words.

Stop the busy beliefs.

Stop the endless mental chatter.

Don't let wordy prayers get in between you and God.

Of course, it is appropriate to pray for yourself, to pray for the world, or to offer your praise and thanksgiving to the divine. But not because God needs Her ego affirmed. Nor does God need an update on the world's needs. Rather, we pray with words out of *our* need, out of the overflow of our often over-full minds and hearts. And when called to pray with words, then it is a gift to do so.

But if words do not naturally flow then let it be. Stop. "Let prayer pray within you, whether you know it or not."

When you "stop" little-p-praying with words, in order to capital-P-Pray without words, a new awareness breaks through, an awareness that Caroline Oakes says is "a new and expanded way of being, into our intuition, into our psyche, and into our bodies. We are changed from the inside out, so to speak."

This change "from the inside out" is the fruit of conscious practice. It is the gift of waking up to our deep Self, rooted in the Ground of Being. And it is the whole point of contemplation. The irony is that for this inner change to take place, we do not need to say the right words, believe the right thoughts or try a bit harder. We might just need to stop.

But what does it practically look like to "stop praying" in order to pray?

A WAY WITHOUT WORDS
CENTERING PRAYER

Spiritual practice is to the mystical life
what food and water is to the body.
Just as we cannot survive very long
without food and water,
we can not survive on the spiritual journey without a
contemplative practice of some sort.

— Wayne Teasdale

If you are going to take contemplative practice seriously, you need a specific method of meditation or prayer. While conventional thought says contemplative practices are ways of feeling "peace," the truth is that meditation is by no means easy or always peaceful, so a good method of meditation will give you some pointers about what to do, and not do, when you sit down and enter your time of practice.

Centering Prayer has been my primary meditation since 2010. I consider Centering Prayer a "mature" meditation practice, mature because it is not a guided meditation. It's a self-directed practice where you are not dependent upon the voice of another to remind you that you are meditating.

The method of Centering Prayer is as follows:

1. Choose a sacred word as the symbol of your intention to consent to God's presence and action within.

2. Sitting comfortably and with eyes closed, settle briefly and silently introduce the sacred word as the symbol of your consent to God's presence and action within.

3. When engaged with your thoughts, return ever-so-gently to the sacred word.

4. At the end of the prayer period, remain in silence with eyes closed for a couple of minutes.

Centering Prayer's power comes from your *intention*: to consent, or say "yes" to God's presence and action within you. We say "yes" by letting go of our thoughts and returning to our sacred word. The word *thoughts* is a technical term in Centering Prayer. A thought is anything that passes the mind's eye, be it an idea, a plan, a vision, a feeling, or an itch on your nose. *Thoughts* in Centering Prayer are the domain of the thinking-feeling-doing-self. But we're after something much deeper: our self that is grounded in Being.

With regular practice, you'll find a diversity of experience. You'll encounter seasons of deep quiet, rest, and interior silence. You'll encounter seasons of boredom and questioning, "Is this meditation doing anything for me? Am I even doing this right?" Sometimes old memories emerge, unwelcomed thoughts, and even past trauma. But as we let go and "return to our sacred word" you'll also encounter *healing*. In Centering Prayer, this inner healing is called *Divine Therapy*. Centerings commitment to "letting go" and surrendering of every *thought*, past memories included, is a profound path of authentic healing.

Grounded in God, Centering Prayer allows us to become who we were before we became who we are not.

As we "let go of thoughts" and "return to our sacred word," we are letting go of our small self, a self that is wrapped up in habitual thinking patterns, limiting belief, and conditioning from the past. As our letting go deepens to surrender, our identity shifts from being rooted in thinking-feeling-doing to being rooted in the Greater Being of life. And as we move from the meditation cushion to the chaos of the world, confronting the storms of life, we realize that we are not alone, we are rooted, grounded, and stabilized in the great Ground of Being.

A meditation community and meditation teacher can be a great help. In my Closer Than Breath community, we often practice Centering Prayer together on Zoom. We gather online, hear a poetic reading and share 20 minutes of silent Centering Prayer together. It's sacred space. After the meditation we enter a time of sharing from the heart. The depth of insight and struggle shared is rich. The quality of sharing is enhanced by the silence we shared in Centering.

How long should you practice meditation? Centering Prayer is generally practiced every day for 20-minutes at a time. If that feels too long at first, it is perfectly fine to begin with just a few minutes and slowly build up as your practice matures. You will become more comfortable with silence and stillness.

The struggle to "find the time" to meditate can be real, and sometimes, born out of egoic resistance. With some Zen wit, some say "*You should sit in meditation every day for 20 minutes. Unless you're too busy. Then you should sit for an hour.*" Ouch. With committed practice, you'll begin to see and feel the fruits of practice in your everyday life and any subtle excuses not to practice will diminish. Many people that commit to a daily sit even experience a kind of magnetic pull to their meditation chair. It is as if your inner Being is waiting to be watered, God is saying "Enough with the endless thinking-feeling-doing, thinking-feeling-doing. Come and Be with Me. I AM here now."

THE EVERYDAY MYSTIC

No spiritual insight or spiritual teacher is better than spiritual practice. And ultimately, everyday life is our practice. If you feel invited to cultivate contemplative consciousness, then honor that call with intentional commitment. No one can do our inner work for us. So the decision is ours to make: will we, will you, consciously feed your being?

The invitation is to get "centered" and to live from your center, a divine Center, in an off-centered world. Gratefully, the fruit of your practice is yours to enjoy: knowing you are one with the Source of joy. Even better, the gift of joy is meant to be shared. Changed from the inside out, we are each invited to bring greater peace and presence into this world that needs more of both.

11

CREATIVITY BY ANY OTHER NAME
Colleen Thomas

"Ever since I was a child, I liked to be quiet." This is how I introduce myself to my spiritual direction cohort. It is true. I love the silence. Growing up, I enjoyed quiet activities like going to the library and reading between the stacks of books. I played the violin although never at a very advanced level but the Suzuki training stuck with me enough to influence a great love of classical music. Now as an adult I'd prefer an evening with Gustavo Dudamel conducting the L.A. Philharmonic to a Beyoncé concert any night. While reading and the symphony are not silence in its truest form, they create for me an interior silence characteristic of the contemplative life. Like prayer, these quiet activities serve to create an atmosphere for contemplation. And contemplation, is in essence, the vocation of the mystic.

I called myself a mystic before I even knew what a mystic was. In my formative spiritual years as I was coming to awareness of the Christian contemplative tradition, my spirituality and creativity were intricately linked and connected. As I was coming to know the mystics, I was also coming to find my voice, both as a writer and at the time, as a singer-songwriter.

I was also a creative long before I had a definition of creativity. Within my interior childhood world, I created worlds. I wrote fictional stories, poetry, prose, and character dialogue. Words gave form to my dreams and desires. In my early twenties and college years, words began to attach themselves to melody, giving a more expansive expression to my longings. I was discovering through music that it is an art to articulate a feeling. To name it. Isn't this why we turn to iconic songs and musicians, because they have the ability to name for us a feeling? In their lyric and composition they risk feeling for us. This is the soul-stirring gift of creatives to this world.

Mystics are like this too, in their daring to see and reflect what it is true. They practice the art of exchanging a perceived reality for an Ultimate Reality and bear the weight of their experiences - pain and suffering, ecstasy or delight. Whatever may come, the mystic and the creative let their hearts break open completely. They live by prophet singer-songwriter Leonard Cohen's poetic expression "Everything has a crack in it that's how the light gets in." And by pop icon Feist's soul baring lyric "my wings are wide, my wings are wide, why carry it inside, why carry it inside." This kind of perceiving takes courage. Mystics and creatives walk daringly. They strip naked in plain sight baring it all, and we can't help not to look away. James Finley, a teacher of mine during my spiritual direction training, is famous for saying, "God protects us from nothing but sustains us in everything." The vocation of the mystic is to face reality, and encounter the Real.

When a seminary professor of mine introduced a young class of hopeful seminarians to Hildegard of Bingen I felt a spark. I don't recall if the professor called her a mystic but Hildegard left a firm and lasting impression on me. This saying of hers, "I am like a feather on the breath of God" included on a long list of quotes from her various works sung like lyrics to my soul. This, I knew, was mysticism.

Hildegard, a fourteenth century German nun and abbess was a mystic because she saw the unity of all things. She saw us as one with God and God as one with the cosmos. She saw the body as one with the spirit and the spirit as one with the soul. She saw the man as one with the woman and the earth as one with us. She also saw brokenness in government and the limitations of power and lived without separating her life of prayer from her practice of speaking truth to power. Hildergard's way embodies what mysticism is in its simplest essence. It is more than an experience of oneness with God and others. It is a prophetic seeing beyond what is to what can be.

Now years later, I often reflect on the need for an expanded canon of who we call mystics. History has limited mystics to monastic or religious figures like Hildegard, and John of the Cross. But John "of A Love Supreme" Coltrane was a mystic too, although certainly not a classical religious contemplative. Meister Coltrane had a spiritual experience awakening him to a new reality of such magnitude that he dedicated his record A Love Supreme to God. That masterpiece is an expression of his experience of divine union. A musical journey chronicling his devotion. This too is the vocation of the mystic - to tell the story.

And yet, one doesn't need to produce a work of musical or literary genius to express meaning and communicate an experience of the holy, do they?

I wish I could say for myself that I've had that kind of A Love Supreme-like outpouring of creativity. I've certainly had holy moments in front of a microphone. Yet I am cautious about limiting creativity to artistic expression in this industrial sense. As more of God's nature is being revealed, as my own receptivity to an evolving image of God expands, and as my heart is being reoriented to the Real, a new understanding of creativity emerges. As I bear witness to the change occurring within me, it strikes me that the very process of transformation is in itself an act of creativity. Being made new is perhaps the greatest creative act of all time.

THE CREATIVE ACT OF NAMING

At its most basic level, creativity is simply the ability to bring to light something new—to see something, or someone, in a new way. The creative person relishes in discovery and exploration, ingenuity and interpretation. Dr. Robert E. Franken in his book Human Motivation defines creativity as "the tendency to generate or recognize ideas." He says:

> *In order to be creative, you need to be able to view things in new ways or from a different perspective. Among other things, you need to be able to generate new possibilities or new alternatives. Tests of creativity measure not only the number of alternatives that people can generate but the uniqueness of those alternatives. the ability to generate alternatives or to see things uniquely does not occur by change; it is linked to other, more fundamental qualities of thinking, such as flexibility, tolerance of ambiguity or unpredictability, and the enjoyment of things heretofore unknown.*

Creativity of this kind is accounted for in both the old and new testaments—God being revealed and recognized in new ways.

Women, often overlooked in scripture are given some pretty significant "first encounters" with God. Mary was the first to be told of God incarnate bearing witness to Jesus' birth in her own womb. And the other Mary, the first to see God resurrected bearing witness to Jesus' risen self. Before both of these Mary's, it is to another women whom God gives an unexpected encounter.

In Genesis, in the midst of Abraham's origin story, we meet Hagar. This woman has been dealt a tough hand. Egyptian born, she's somehow become the possession of Abraham, enslaved and living away from her people. At the mercy of her master's wife's barrenness, Hagar is given to Abraham like cattle to bear a child to be his heir. Having submitted herself to her mistress' will, Hagar becomes pregnant. Like most plots of human will, the successful plan does not lead to joyous times and Hagar's mistress envies Hagar's fruitful womb. As a result, Hagar is subjected to some unidentified form of abuse at the hand of her mistress and so she runs to safety in the desert. It is here, driven away by pride, patriarchy, and fear from the captivity she calls home, Hagar finds herself alone. Then God appears to her.

And he said, "Hagar, slave of Sarai, where have you come from, and where are you going?" "I'm running away from my mistress Sarai," she answered. Then the angel of the Lord told her, "Go back to your mistress and submit to her." The angel added, "I will increase your descendants so much that they will be too numerous to count." The angel of the Lord also said to her: "You are now pregnant and you will give birth to a son. You shall name him Ishmael, for the Lord has heard of your misery; **So she named the Lord who spoke to her, 'You are El-roi' [the God who sees me]; for she said,** *'I have now seen the One who sees me.* **[Have I really seen God and remained alive after seeing him?']**

This woman Hagar, is actually the first person recorded in scripture to name God. In the midst of her self-selected exile, she has a direct experience of God, who speaks directly to her plight, and Hagar names God—El-Roi, The God Who Sees.

In the chapter that follows, we read the account of Abram receiving a new name, Abraham. And Abraham, like his predecessor Hagar, renames God El-Shaddai. Hundreds of years later, we meet the murderous zealot Saul who also has a direct experience of God and emerges from his divine blindness to a new name, Paul, and to a new vision of a loving, inclusive, and non-violent God. While there is no account of Hagar herself receiving a new name, we can imagine that having the experience of this kind of encounter with God, something new is also born within her.

These scriptural examples reveal that not only do we receive a new image of God as a result of a direct experience, we begin to receive a new image of ourselves. There is a mutual change in character. As we encounter God anew, our own identity shifts. When we come to see God through the lens of a new identity, God takes on new character and this the whole way we see ourselves and the world begins to change. This remaking, renaming and revisioning of the world is the mystical vocation of the mystic. And who better to express a vision for a new world than the artists.

THE VOCATION OF THE MYSTIC

"The mystics are artists, and the stuff in which they work is most often human life. They want to heal the disharmony between the actual and the real: and since, in the white-hot radiance of that faith, hope, and charity which burns in them, they discern such a reconciliation to be possible, they are able to work for it with a singleness of purpose and an invincible optimism denied to other men."

Although Evelyn Underhill quoted above doesn't use the word "men" here in a gendered sense, it's still striking to read in the context of considering this first great creative act of a woman naming God. In Hagar's imagining of a new name and a new way of being in her own world she welcomes herself into the canon of mystics.

Imagination has the ability to create a world beyond what can be seen. It is our imagination that enables us to see a world not based on experience but hope. In braving the encounter with Ultimate Reality, the mystic gains a sight beyond earthly vision. Like Hagar, the mystic can now see what lies just on the other side of incomprehensible. The mystic lives as one waking from a dream with a holy desperation to experience that place where dream and reality converge and conjure vapor into substance. The mystic lives in liminal spaces that call what is already-but-not-yet Real.

How does she do this?

AWAKENING TO SEEING THE NEW

"At the centre there is a stillness which even you are not able to break. There, the rhythm of your duration is one with the rhythm of the Universal Life. There, your essential self exists: the permanent being which persists through and behind the flow and change of your conscious states... Turn your consciousness inward to it deliberately. Retreat to that point whence all the various lines of your activities flow, and to which at last they must return."

The ability to see beyond appearances doesn't necessarily come in times of contemplative prayer, but rather by way of them. Evelyn Underhill describes the practice of contemplation as "unrelaxed intention." This understanding does much to thwart common beliefs that meditation and contemplation are in and of themselves acts of peaceful rest. Maintaining a vision, holding on to what God reveals in times of distress requires practice and much intention.

The Hebrews believe in a concept called Midrash, a form of story-telling Rabbis used to fill in the gaps (so to speak) of inconsistencies found in scripture. Midrash became an important practice of Jewish literature. Through midrash, we are invited into an imaginative way of reading scripture "between the lines" and we can hear the missing voice of Hagar after she returns to her home in captivity. The task before her now is to live as though God sees her and through midrash we can imagine that she does this for many more years. She returns to her master and mistress able to live beyond whatever abuse may have awaited and attended her upon her return. She gives birth to Ishmael, who grows up to a certain age where he is old enough to be able to "mock" his now arrived, younger half-brother, Isaac. Hagar's mistress continues for many years to hold her in contempt.

What the written story does tell us is that some years later, Hagar's son Ishmael is now perceived to be a threat to her mistress who commands Hagar and child be cast out. Abraham, though in distress, does not advocate for Hagar and with assurance from God sends the mother and his child away at his wife's request.

So Abraham rose early in the morning, and took bread and a skin of water, and gave it to Hagar, putting it on her shoulder, along with the child, and sent her away. And she departed, and wandered about in the wilderness of Beer-sheba.

When the water in the skin was gone, she cast the child under one of the bushes. 16 Then she went and sat down opposite him a good way off, about the distance of a bow-shot; for she said, 'Do not let me look on the death of the child.' And as she sat opposite him, she lifted up her voice and wept. And God heard the voice of the boy; and the angel of God called to Hagar from heaven, and said to her, 'What troubles you, Hagar? Do not be afraid; for God has heard the voice of the boy where he is. Come, lift up the boy and hold him fast with your hand, for I will make a great nation of him.' Then God opened her eyes, and she saw a well of water. She went, and filled the skin with water, and gave the boy a drink. God was with the boy, and he grew up; he lived in the wilderness, and became an expert with the bow. He lived in the wilderness of Paran; and his mother got a wife for him from the land of Egypt.

It is not necessary to imagine that Hagar lives well, only that she endures. She was able to live with a dignity and a sense of purpose not offered her at the hands of others. She was able to see herself as God sees her, not as she was seen by people who owned, used and discarded her. Under the watchful eye of God, she prevails. She mothered, she created a future for her son, she found him a wife, she lived as one who God had seen in a world that treated her as a disposable commodity.

It is no light task to hold onto a vision of God in a world that shows little sign of God's affection. It is the creative vocation of the mystic not to break faith with what they have seen to be true. To do so requires much practice. The primary discipline of the mystic is to return with intention to what is True and to maintain this connection to Reality at all costs. It is the practice of returning to the center where "there is a stillness which you cannot break." There at the center is the memory of oneness with the God who sees. There at the center is your real name, along with the seat of all of your understanding, wisdom and knowledge. There at the center is where the mystic begins to think and see as God does and access the ability to create a new world, a world in which there is a future and a hope. This is creativity at it finest.

MYSTICISM AT THE MARGINS

Artists, aware of a more vivid and beautiful world than other men, are always driven by their love and enthusiasm to attempt the expression, the bringing into manifestation of those deeper significances of form, sound, rhythm which they have been able to apprehend... a desire to fix within the time-order, and share with other men, the vision by which they were possessed... that it may draw from this direct experience of Reality a new intensity wherewith to handle the world of things; and remake it, or it lease some little bit of it, 'nearer to the heart's desire.

Remaking the world, for those on the margins like Hagar, is not mere creative passion. Barbara Holmes says that when crisis is one's reality, contemplation is "neither the result of spiritual seeking nor the voluntary entry into meditative spaces. It is a cracking open, the rupture and shattering of self, community, expectations, and presumptions about how the world works." Mysticism then, is also an act of survival. It is to act anew, like Hagar; to act as if God sees you, regardless of the gaze of contempt around you.

The mystic is always on the margins acting as one who has seen God and living as one who dares to tell that story. To share that kind of vision with others does require that you paint a masterpiece, write a novel, nor compose a symphony. If such an act of industry should be born out of your devotion, let it be. But if your one great act of creative devotion would be to surrender yourself to the adoration of the holy in yourself, and others, this too has the creative power to change worlds.

AUTHOR BIOS

Aurelia Dávila Pratt

Rev. Aurelia Dávila Pratt is the lead pastor of Peace of Christ Church, a radically loving community in Round Rock, Texas. Named by Sojourners as one of "Ten Christian Women Shaping the Church in 2022", Aurelia is also the author of A Brown Girl's Epiphany: Reclaim Your Intuition and Step into Your Power. Her writings have been featured in Progressing Spirit, Good Faith Media, Sojourners, the Alliance of Baptists, Baptist Women in Ministry, and the Austin American Statesman. Find her on Instagram @revaureliajoy or visit her website: www.revaureliajoy.com

Colleen Thomas

Colleen Thomas is an ordained minister, Spiritual Director, writer and podcast host. A longtime practitioner of Centering Prayer, she serves as the Diversity Outreach Coordinator for Contemplative Outreach Ltd. She worked in television in Los Angeles for 15 years before relocating to her hometown of Washington, D.C. where she now serves as the Pastor of Spiritual Formation at Peace Fellowship Church. In 2020 she founded Soul Care LA to offer contemplative prayer groups, workshops, and retreats for young professionals, creatives, and BIPOC communities. Colleen holds an MA in Theology and Art from Fuller Theological Seminary and a certificate in the Art of Spiritual Direction

& Retreat Leadership from the Spirituality Center at Mount Saints Mary's in Los Angeles, CA.

Tim Burnette

Tim writes and teaches in philosophy, theology, cosmology, and decolonial mysticism. He earned his doctorate from Claremont School of Theology, where he studied process metaphysics and compassion. He has hosted the Theopoetics Podcast and currently curates Way Collective, which is a contemplative community for love and liberation in Santa Barbara, CA. He is a partner, father, musician, athlete, and avid reader. He agrees with Kurt Vonnegut that you can see all kinds of things from the edge that you can't see from the center. Although...sometimes it helps to be centered out on the edge as well.

Keith Kristich

Keith Kristich is the founder of Closer Than Breath, an online interspiritual community dedicated to the teaching and practice of contemplative prayer. As a writer and retreat leader, Keith brings an interspiritual approach to spiritual teaching, integrating wisdom from various contemplative traditions while highlighting the often-forgotten mystical teachings of Christianity. He is a commissioned teacher of Centering Prayer through Contemplative Outreach, trained with the Shalem Institute for Spiritual Formation, and a certified teacher of the Enneagram, and meditation.

Caroline Oakes

Caroline Oakes is author of Practice the Pause: Jesus' Contemplative Practice, New Brain Science, and What It Means to Be Fully Human, published by Broadleaf Books. Her essays have been published at On Being, The Huffington Post, and her bimonthly "Mind & Spirit" column in The Bucks County Herald. She has a master's degree in ascetical theology from the General Theological Seminary of the Episcopal Church and is trained in teaching contemplative practice and meditation by Shalem Institute for Spiritual Formation and Mindful Schools, Inc. She lives in Annapolis, Maryland and can be reached on Instagram @carolineoakes.

Tia Norman

Tia Norman is a teacher and guide specializing in spirituality and practices anchored in the mystical teachings of the Christian contemplative tradition. She serves as Pastor of

Awakenings, Inc., a contemplative community based in Houston, Texas and helps individuals and communities discover ways to weave contemplative practices and teachings into their lives and context as the owner of A Contemplative Space LLC.

Brandan Robertson

Rev. Brandan Robertson is a noted author, activist, and public theologian, working at the intersections of spirituality, sexuality, and social renewal. He serves as the Pastor of Sunnyside Reformed Church in New York City. He's widely known as the "TikTok Pastor", with a vast digital reach of over 250k followers and 6 million views engaging his inclusive theological digital content. He's also the host of the Devout and Out podcast, featuring conversations with leading queer spiritual leaders. his academic pursuits, Robertson acquired a Bachelor of Arts in Pastoral Ministry and Biblical Studies from Moody Bible Institute, an Master of Theological Study from Iliff School of Theology, and an Master of Arts in Political Science and Public Administration from

Eastern Illinois University. He's presently pursuing a PhD in Biblical Studies at Drew University. He currently resides in New York City.

Benjamin Perry

Rev. Benjamin Perry is Minister of Outreach and Media Strategy at Middle Church, and author of Cry, Baby: Why Our Tears Matter, published by Broadleaf Books, May 2023. An award-winning writer, his work focuses on the intersection of religion and politics. Their writing can be found in outlets like The Atlantic, The Washington Post, Slate, The Huffington Post, Sojourners, Bustle and Motherboard and he has appeared on MSNBC, Al Jazeera, and NY1. They hold a degree in psychology from SUNY Geneseo and a Masters of Divinity from Union Theological Seminary. He is married to Erin Mayer, they live in Maine with his brother and best friend. They are the editor of the Queer Faith photojournalism series, curator of an art exhibit by the same name, and a passionate advocate for building Church that lives into God's blessed queerness. His two proudest achievements are skydiving with his grandmother and winning first prize in his seminary drag show.

Jen Wood

Jen Wood is the co-founder of Expansion Lab, an innovative transformational and executive coaching firm. Jen specializes in fostering personal and professional growth, enhancing leadership skills, and nurturing individuals. Jen co-founded Redemption Church in Costa Mesa, Ca and has a rich background in spiritual leadership, personal growth and community building. Her work at Expansion Lab empowers leaders, teams, couples and individuals to achieve their goals and attain meaningful success through holistic growth, sustainable change and performance improvement.

Phil Wood

Phil Wood is the co-founder of Expansion Lab and an executive coach. With expertise in leadership development, personal transformation, and organizational growth, Phil helps individuals, couples and teams navigate complex challenges and drive success. He specializes in developing transformation, enhancing emotional intelligence, and building cohesive teams. He co-founded and was lead Pastor of Redemption Church in Costa Mesa, Ca and has led multiple organizations. At Expansion Lab, he empowers individuals and leaders to unlock their full potential, achieve their goals, and achieve extraordinary results.

Shawn T. Ellison

Shawn T. Ellison, MA, RN, is a Catholic mystic, contemplative writer, spiritual director, and registered nurse. He is an aspiring member of the Secular Order of the Discalced Carmelites (OCDS), and is passionate about guiding spiritual seekers to an abiding union with God through grace. By contemplative vocation, he experientially identifies with the mystical lineage of St. Teresa of Avila, St. John of the Cross, and Bernadette Roberts. He resides in the San Francisco Bay Area with his wife and daughter. Lastly, Shawn may be contacted for spiritual direction and collaborative inquiries at shawn@contemplativevision.com.

Carl Amouzou (he/his/him)

In Mark's gospel, there is a scene where a father, who is desperate to see his son healed, says to Jesus, "I believe; help my unbelief!" This proclamation has been at the center of Carl's journey, paradoxically following Jesus in belief and unbelief. It has been a call to live in the liminal spaces of life: multiethnic, multicultural, settler, and immigrant. Carl rediscovered his faith when he learned it was okay to live in the tension of hope and doubt. Learning to grow in liminal spaces is to understand "you belong everywhere, you belong nowhere, you belong to yourself" to paraphrase the late great Maya Angelou.

Carl is a spiritual nomad, creative, storyteller, and pastor.

For the past 18 years, Carl has been on a journey of starting faith communities and equipping leaders for the future Church. Carl holds a MAT from Fuller Theological Seminary and a BA in Bible and Pastoral Ministry from Pacific Rim Christian College.

Kevin Sweeney

Kevin was co-founder and lead pastor of Imagine Church for almost ten years. He is the host of podcast "The Church Needs Therapy" and is a best selling author. His two books are *The Making of a Mystic* and *The Joy of Letting Go*. He is also co-founder of Rooftop Alliance, and ecosystem for celebrating and funding change makers, based out of New York City. He currently lives and surfs In Honolulu with his wife and co-founder of Imagine, Christine, and their two kids, True and Mikayla.

Carmen Acevedo Butcher, PhD

Carmen Acevedo Butcher is an internationally acclaimed speaker, author, educator, and poet. An award-winning translator, she has made accessible works of Early Modern French, German, Latin, Middle English, and Old English, by writers including the seventeenth-century friar Brother Lawrence, Hildegard of Bingen, Mechthild of Magdeburg, the Cloud's Anonymous, Julian of Norwich, and tenth-century Benedictine monk Ælfric of Eynsham. Carmen's translation of Cloud of Unknowing (Shambhala Pocket Library, 2018) won an Author of the Year award from the Georgia Writers Association in 2010. Her tenth book, Practice of the Presence, is a revolutionary translation of the wisdom of Brother Lawrence, releasing in 2022 from Broadleaf Books.

BOOKS REFERENCED

David Anderson, *The Rev.*, *Finding Your Soul blogpost*, *"What Does It Mean to Repent?*(February 27, 2023. https://findingyoursoul.com /2023/02/what-does-it-mean-to-repent/)

Edward J. Anton, Repentance: *A Cosmic Shift of Mind and Heart* (New York, NY: Discipleship Publications, 2005)

Hildegard of Bingen, *Selected Writings* (Westminster, London: Penguin Books Limited, 2005)

Cynthia Bourgeault, *Contemplative Prayer and Inner Awakening* (New York, NY: Cowley Publications, 2004)

Cynthia Bourgeault, *Wisdom Jesus: Transforming Heart and Mind* (Boston, MA: Shambhala, 2008)

Brother David, *Monastic Studies* (Pine City, NY: Mount Saviour Monastery,1969)

Meister Eckhart, *The Essential Sermons* (New York/Mahwah NJ: Paulist Press, 1981)

T. S. Eliot, *Collected Poems, 1909-1962* (The Centenary Edition) (New York, NY: Harcourt Brace & Company, 1991)

Feist, "Feel It All." The Reminder, Arts & Crafts, Cherrytree, Interscope, Polydor, 2007.

Robert Franken, *Human Motivation,* (Belmont, CA: Thomson/Wadsworth, 2007)

Madame Jeanne Guyon, *Intimacy with Jesus: Verse by Verse From the Song of Songs* (Scotts Valley, CA: CreateSpace Independent Publishing Platform, 2016)

Abraham Joshua Heschel, *Moral Grandeur And Spiritual Audacity* (New York, NY: Farrar, Strauss and Giroux, 1996)

Abraham Joshua Heschel, *The Sabbath* (New York, NY: Farrar, Straus and Giroux, 1975)

Barbara Holmes, *Crisis Contemplation: Healing The Wounded Village* (Albuquerque, NM: CAC Publishing, 2021)

Bell Hooks, *All About Love: New Visions* (New York, NY: William Morrow, 2000)

Bell Hooks, *Outlaw Culture: Resisting Interpretations* (New York, NY: Routledge Classics, 1994)

St. John Of The Cross, *A Spiritual Canticle Of The Soul And The Bridegroom Of Christ* (New York, NY: Magisterium Press, 2015)

Thomas Keating, *The Human Condition: Contemplation and Transformation* (New York, NY: Paulist Press, 1999)

Catherine Keller, *From a Broken Web: Separation, Sexism and Self* (Boston, MA: Beacon Press, 1988)

Dacher Keltner, *Awe: The New Science of Everyday Wonder and How It Can Transform Your Life* (New York, NY: Penguin Books, 2023)

Grace Ji Sun Kim, *Re-imagining Spirit: Wind, Breath, and Vibration* (Eugene, OR: Cascade Books, 2019)

Krishnananda, *The Chhandogya Upanishad* (Himalayas, India: Divine Life Society, Shivanandanagar, Distt. Tehri-Garhwal, U.P.,1984)

Brother Lawrence of the Resurrection, Carmen Acevedo Butcher, *Practice Of The Presence* (Minneapolis, MN: Broadleaf Books, 2022)

Thomas Merton, *New Seeds of Contemplation* (New York, NY: New Directions, 1961)

Thomas Merton, *Raids On The Unspeakable* (New York, NY: New Directions, 1964)

Kathleen Norris, *The Quotidian Mysteries: Laundry, Liturgy and "Women's Work"* (New York/Mahwah, NJ: Paulist Press, 1998)

Henri Nouwen, *Walking With Henri Nouwen: A Reflective Journey* (New York, NY: Paulist Press, 2003)

Henri Nouwen, *The Wounded Healer: Ministry In Contemporary Society* (New York: NY Image Double Day, 1972)

Caroline Oakes, *Practice the Pause: Jesus' Contemplative Practice, New Brain Science, and What It Means To Be Fully Human* (Indianapolis, IN: Broadleaf Books, 2023)

Rashid Osmani, *In the Footsteps of Rumi...: Modern Verse with a Whiff of the Master's Fragrance* (Bloomington, IN: Balboa Press, 2013)

Mary Oliver, guest. *On Being With Krista Tippet.* On Being Studios, 2022, https://onbeing.org/programs/mary-oliver-i-got-saved-by-the-beauty-of-the-world/

Lama Rod Owens, *Love and Rage: The Path of Liberation Through Anger* (Berkeley, CA: North Atlantic Books, 2020)

A. T. Robertson, *Word Pictures in the New Testament—2 Corinthians* (Grand Rapids, MO: Christian Classics Ethereal Library, November 14, 2014)

Richard Rohr, *Falling Upward: Spirituality for the Two Halves of Life* (San Francisco, CA: Jossey Bass, 2011)

Richard Rohr, *Franciscan Media blogpost, How Can Anyone Pray 'Always'?,* (June 11, 2020 https://www.franciscanmedia.org/francisc an-spirit-blog/how-can-anyone-pray-always-2/#google_vignette)

David Rowe and Robert Schulmann, *Einstein on Politics: His Private Thoughts and Public Stands on Nationalism* (Princeton, NJ: Princeton University Press, 2007)

Chief siʔałꝺ, Duwamish Tribe, *Who We Are,* (2018 https://www.du wamishtribe.org/chief-siahl)

Mirabai Starr, *Ordinary Mysticism: Your Life As Sacred ground* (San Francisco, CA: HarperOne, 2024)

Wayne Teasdale, *The Mystic Heart: Discovering a Universal Spirituality in the World's Religions* (Novato, CA: New World Library, 1999)

The Gospel of Thomas. https://www.biblicalarchaeology.org/daily/biblical-topics/bible-versions-and-translations/the-gospel-of-thomas-114-sayings-of-jesus

Howard Thurman, *The Sound Of The Genuine,* (Baccalaureate Ceremony,

May 4, 1980, Spelman College, Atlanta, Georgia, Commencement Address)

Andrew Travers, *How Thomas Keating Launched a Global Interfaith Movement from a Snowmass Monastery* (Aspen Times, October 31, 2019.)

Evelyn Underhill, *The Cloud of Unknowing: A Book Of Contemplation The Which Is Called The Cloud Of Unknowing, In The Which A Soul Is Oned With God* (Cleveland, OH: Alicia Editions, 2020)

Evelyn Underhill, *Mysticism: A Study in Nature and Development of Spiritual Consciousness* (Mineola, NY: Dover Publications, 2002)

Evelyn Underhill, *Practical Mysticism: A Little Book For Normal People* (Scotts Valley, CA: CreateSpace Independent Publishing Platform, 2013)

To contact Kevin Sweeney for speaking engagements,
please visit www.kevinsweeneynow.com.

Many Voices. One Message.

quoir.com